Java™ in Practice

Java™ in Practice

Design styles and idioms for effective Java

Nigel Warren
Digital Bridges Ltd

Philip Bishop
Eveque Systems Ltd

Addison-Wesley

Harlow, England ● Reading, Massachusetts ● Menlo Park, California

New York ● Don Mills, Ontario ● Amsterdam ● Bonn ● Sydney ● Singapore

Tokyo ● Madrid ● San Juan ● Milan ● Mexico City ● Seoul ● Taipei

© Addison Wesley Longman Limited 1999

Addison Wesley Longman Limited
Edinburgh Gate
Harlow
Essex CM20 2JE
England

and Associated Companies throughout the World.

Cover designed by ODB Design & Illustration, Reading
Typeset in Stone Sans and Serif by 43
Printed and bound in the United States of America

First published 1999

ISBN 0-201-36065-9

British Library Cataloguing-in-Publication Data
A catalogue record for this book is available from the British Library

Library of Congress Cataloging-in-Publication Data
Warren, Nigel.
    Java in practice : design styles and idioms for effective Java /
Nigel Warren, Phil Bishop.
        p.   cm.
    Includes bibliographical references and index.
    ISBN 0-201-36065-9
    1. Java (Computer program language)   I. Bishop, Phil.   II. Title.
QA76.73.J38W367   1999
005.13'3--dc21   98-44138
                                                              CIP

Contents

Introduction

The design of the Java platform reflects a shift in priorities in both computer languages and systems design. This shift has brought about changes that have had very subtle yet profound effects as the use of the Java platform has steadily matured.

One key change has been that Java has reversed the trend of object-oriented (OO) languages becoming increasingly complex. It is Java's relative simplicity that makes it so clear at expressing the solutions to programming problems, making it a wonderful language both to learn and to teach. This simplicity allows us to lift our gaze from the world of language constructs, to the wider and much richer world of object-oriented design and language idioms.

What we have tried to do in this book is to set down some of our Java experience in the manner of a discussion; which is really about how to solve programming problems with the Java platform, using a set of design principles.

It is a discussion about how the design is affected by the use of Java and about how certain patterns that appear commonly in software can be reflected into the Java world as idioms. Occasionally we have distilled our experience into Java rules, design principles, or tips.

Java rules simply must be adhered to. We do not define them, they are normally defined in the Java Language Specification, but we introduce them when they become salient to the discussion. We have assumed that the more obvious Java rules are known, leaving us the more esoteric ones that form the "hard walls" that mark out the edges of the design space in which we are working.

The design principles outline ideas that are generally going to help you to make better Java software across the board. They are not always going to apply but we have found them extremely useful in a number of cases.

You might choose to use the tips to guide your thinking and approach to solutions. If you find yourself in a corner, but it has the shape of a situation that we have already described, it might be useful to apply a tip.

As with all things, please keep in mind that blindly learning and applying these rules, or copying the code examples, is really not what this book is all about. What is most important is following and appreciating the arguments that support the decisions that we make in the development of this discussion.

You may not even agree with some of the solutions that we propose, but we hope that you can see the point in most. The key is to see the process of the design and stated objectives of the system being fulfilled via the use of Java. When you come to apply these ideas in your own work, in almost every case, there will be subtle forces at work that we cannot consider in general forms and so these ideas and principles may apply in slightly different ways.

For us it is this constant subtle variation that is the real joy of developing software in an iterative manner. It is the opportunity to mold a design, so that it slowly becomes a better and better "fit" for the problem that we are given, that is illuminating and the source of a never-ending set of new ideas.

In keeping with the philosophy of simplicity, this book is divided into two parts. The first three chapters introduce the three fundamentals – the "lingua franca" – of object-oriented design in the form of encapsulation, inheritance, and polymorphism.

Only when we understand these key concepts can we begin to work productively with the idioms that we present over the course of the remainder of the book. You will find that these basic ideas are mapped and remapped into various forms as we discuss the solutions to a very varied set of programming problems in the forms of "real-world" examples and occasionally "real bizarre" examples.

Recently it has become popular to look upon the Java libraries in the same way that hardware designers look upon the chips that they use to produce a computer design. Hence the Java libraries become the packages that we must "wire" together to produce our new software systems. This is an incredibly powerful model that encourages global reuse and commoditization of these software components.

So given this model and its benefits, how does this book stand? In essence it is a set of suggestions about how we wire these components together to create new products and software solutions. What is really important is not the chips, or even the wire, it is the how and the why of the design.

Enjoy...

Notes for navigating the contents

This book is put together so that it can be read directly from the first chapter to the last. However, certain readers may choose to move around the material in such a way that items less familiar to them can be learned more quickly. Here are a few suggested "route maps" for various readers.

All readers should understand the various types of icons that we are using to denote the Java rules, design principles, and tips.

If you are not familiar with UML you may like to read the appendix that describes the subset of UML notation that we use, or you may like to just press on and refer to this section when you come across symbols or annotations with which you are unfamiliar.

The first three chapters of this book are intended to introduce the foundations of object-oriented programming in Java. These may not be appealing initially for programmers already familiar with the OO principles, but we urge these readers most strongly to review these chapters at a later time.

There are a lot of ideas in this book, and readers may find that taking a break and actually applying these ideas in Java code will make things more concrete in their minds, and give a better foundation for reading further chapters; we call these "code breaks." Again we have suggested key places to take code breaks, but this is obviously something that readers may wish to apply rigorously at the end of each chapter, for example, or as and when the need arises.

C and Pascal programmers' route
Chapters 1–3
Long code break to apply the principles
Chapters 4–5
Code break
Chapters 6–11 with code breaks
Review Chapters 1–3

C++ programmers familiar with exceptions' route
Chapter 4
Skim Chapter 5 noting differences
Chapters 6–11 with code breaks
Chapters 1–3

C++ programmers unfamiliar with exceptions' route
Chapters 4–11 with code breaks
Chapters 1–3

SmallTalk programmers' route
Chapters 10–11
Chapters 4–9
Chapters 1–3

CLOS programmers' anti-route
Chapters 11–1

Object architects and designers whose target language is Java will benefit most from reading the book cover to cover and subsequently referring as required.

Icon bullet points

Throughout this book we use the following icons to emphasize Java rules, design principles, and tips.

 Java Rule – absolute language rules.

 Design Principle – guidelines for improving designs.

 Tip – useful language and coding tips.

Acknowledgments

We would like to thank the review team of Dan Creswell, Simon Roberts, Steve Bullimore, Adam Polczyk, Colin Anderson, and Kevlin Henney; a special thank-you goes to Tim Russell for his constantly insightful and helpful comments, and technical reviewing skills.

We can now be sure, thanks to the review team, that any remaining mistakes are completely our doing!

The long-suffering Sally Mortimore and Fiona Kinnear, our editors at Addison Wesley Longman, deserve a special mention along with the whole Addison Wesley team for their help and support throughout.

Here is a list of people, grouped by their current affiliation, whose help, insight, tolerance, and guidance we really appreciate. Everyone below has contributed in at least some small way to making this book possible and in some cases, we could not have made it without them. Apologies for any omissions.

Jeff Farr, Ian Henning, Iain Marshall, Phil Harris, Mike Hoskins, Patrick Farley, and Clare Bradford at BT Labs.

Dave Pinnington, Andy Davidson, Martin Hogg, and Jerry West at Sun Microsystems.

Bill Walker, Bob Gilson, Elizabeth Shimmin, Bob Bridges, Eric Corbett, Rob Day, Robert Woodley, Phil Sully, Steve Tillotson, John Lewis, Des Ward, and Tyrone Howe at QA Training and Consulting.

James Love and Dominique Gloagen at British Telecom.

Simon Robinson, Dominic Badger, and Malcolm Appleby at Cellnet.

Martin Easterbrook at Communication Arts Ltd.

Adrian Jones at Versant Object Techology.

John Fallows at Oracle.

Liu Jian Guo, Philippa Mason, and John Moore at the Imperial College of Science, Technology and Medicine.

Yukoh Matsumoto at TOPS Corporation.

Philippe Dal at Cray-SGI and the Université Libre de Bruxelles.

Martin Ellis, Mark Taylor, Jim VanPeursem, John Whalen, and Mark Vandenbrink at Motorola.

Dave Birch, Stuart Fisk, and Gloria Benson at Hyperion Consulting.

Anthony Flynn, Martin Chapman, and Mike Swainston-Rainford at Iona Technologies.

Chris Smith at Ericsson R&D Labs.

Hartmut Wolf at Beta Research.

Channing Walton at Cannon Research Centre Europe.

Neill McQuillin at IBM Germany.

Keith Allwood, Tony Bedford, Bill Blunn, Paddy Byers, Pam Carter, Francis Charig, Peter Davidson, Adrian Dawson, Jay Foad, Andy Hayward, Stuart Hill, Chris Hinsley, Andy Humphreys, and Tim Renouf at Tao Systems.

Bruce Froehlich at FHT Research.

Per Selbekk, Greg Cutler, Mazen Traboulsi, Rob Bettinson, Andy Smith, Bill Ray and Richard Osbaldeston at MacUk-SwissCom. Hey we're just having way too much fun!

Rob Hemmings and Rose Kozik at Rob&Rose.com

Jonathan Woolf.

Andrew Cunningham at Air New Zealand.

John D. Mitchell and Jill Steinberg at *Java World*, along with their readers who provided valuable feedback to Phil's articles.

Most of all...

   ...Nige would like to thank *Mandy*, *Clare*, *Chris*, *Ken*, and *Hazel*.

   ...Phil would like to thank *Stella* and *Daisy*.

The publishers wish to thank the following for permission to reproduce the following copyright material.

Addison Wesley Longman, Reading, USA
E. Gamma/R. Helm/R. Johnson/J. Vlissides, *Design Patterns* (pages 185, 127) © 1995 by Addison Wesley Publishing Company. Reprinted by permission of Addison Wesley Longman.

Sybex Inc., California, USA
Text from Simon Roberts & Philip Heller: *Java 1.1 Certification Study Guide*.

1 Encapsulation

Encapsulation in software

Extending encapsulated systems

Packages

Inner classes

Introduction

Examples of encapsulation can be found almost everywhere that you look, certainly in the "modern world". So before we start to talk specifically about software, it is interesting to look at some uses of encapsulation in the "outside" world.

We would expect that almost all of the readers of this book will be familiar with hand-held video cameras. When you buy a camera of almost any type, the manufacturer will warranty the product and fix it if it goes wrong for a given period. The warranty also states that there are "no user serviceable parts inside." In fact, if the camera is opened, the warranty will be void.

So the deal is, if you promise not to open the camera case, it is the responsibility of the manufacturer to fix what is inside the case. This is great because it means that we do not have to worry or know about what is inside the camera. The camera encapsulates all of the miniature electronics and mechanisms that enable it to record the video images and sounds onto the tape. You do not get to see what goes on inside the camera which is probably a good idea considering the complexity of the internals of these devices.

In computer hardware we are beginning to come to the same conclusions. Up until recently, the standard model of a computer had "user serviceable" parts in the form of replaceable hard drives and plug-in boards. This model is changing owing to the problems of updating the hardware and the inherent cost involved in maintaining hardware in this form. "Network Computers" (NC) which encapsulate all of this behavior, often without any moving parts, in a "sealed box," have been developed to solve many of these problems. A Network Computer is sometimes called a "commodity model" product. There are two main reasons for this. In the workplace we want to use our time solving the problems of our business, not maintaining our computing equipment. At home we may not have the skills or the inclination required to swap boards, disk drives, and so on.

In both cases we are basically saying that it is not our job to maintain the hardware. For example, most of us would not consider trying to fix our own video recorder, microwave, washing machine, and so on.

Using this model, if the item breaks we take it to someone who does have the skills to fix it, or we simply write it off, throw it away, and buy a new one.

Given all of this experience from the world of physical devices, be they video cameras, mobile phones, network computers, or any other "commodity device," we may be wise to apply the principles of encapsulation to our software.

Encapsulation in software

You may be familiar with the terms "information hiding" or "data hiding," which are also forms of encapsulation; however, in object-oriented software design we can not only hide the information or data, but also the methods that operate on these data, and so we use the more general term encapsulation.

In Java there are special keywords that enable us to use encapsulation to "seal the box" of our software – every class is a "box" and we can close parts of the box so that these parts are not "user serviceable," that is, hiding the internal data representation of that class, by using the keyword private.

In the example below class Customer has a private BankAccount, which is a good thing, not only in the implementation of a software design. By making BankAccount a private instance variable other classes cannot get their hands on a Customer object's BankAccount and ultimately their cash!

```java
public class Customer
{
  private BankAccount account_;
  //public methods
}
```

This example is the simplest form of encapsulation – hiding the internal implementation details of a class. However, if the requirements of the system were to be able to determine a person's current account balance from a Customer object, you could simply add a public method to class Customer which returns their current balance.

```java
public double getCurrentBalance()
{
  return account_.currentBalance();
}
```

By providing the public method getCurrentBalance() we are encapsulating class Customer's use of a BankAccount object – or to put it another way, Customer is dependent on BankAccount, but clients of Customer are not. Reducing dependencies between classes is an important aspect of object-oriented design, a theme which recurs throughout this book.

There are some examples in the AWT where these basic rules are not followed. The java.awt.Point class, for instance, has both its x and y fields defined as:

```
public int x;
public int y;
```

This produces two types of dependencies, which are not present in the previous example.

The first dependency is that other classes can make direct access to the state of the Point class. Our understanding of the rationale for this design decision was that the Point class must be as fast as possible; however, there are ways of retaining performance without introducing these dependencies, and we will say more about this later on.

The second dependency is on the type of the variable. That is, all of the using classes (sometimes these are called client classes) are not only accessing the state of the Point class directly but must also write code that assumes the type of the field. For example, if we had made account_ public in our Customer class you could quite easily write code that becomes dependent on class BankAccount's accessibility.

```
public void noEncapsulation( Customer cust )
{
    BankAccount acc=cust.account_;
}
```

If you later changed the implementation of class Customer so it no longer used a BankAccount object, all references to the publicly accessible account_ would no longer compile, resulting in a considerable amount of reworking – this is the dependency mentioned earlier.

Back to the class Point...

In a multi-threaded system it is possible for two or more other objects to access an object of the Point class at the same time. By breaking encapsulation and allowing clients of the class Point to directly access its internal state there is a strong possibility that undefined behavior will result. Consider the code below, in the context of a multi-threaded system, where the client intends to increment both x and y coordinates:

```
point.x++;
point.y++;
```

If two objects are running in separate threads, both share a reference to the point object and perform this code. Both will read as though the x and y values for the point will be incremented whereas the value of both items may be doubly incremented. This is a very simple case, lying at the start of a whole raft of problems. By not encapsulating your code you are laying your software open to this and many other more complex and nasty bugs. Because Java is inherently multi-threaded it is very important to consider these issues; however, it is well beyond the scope of this chapter to look at this issue in more detail. We strongly recommend that you read Doug Lea's book on *Concurrent Programming in Java* (1997) which covers the topic in fine detail.

Aim to make all of your instance variables private and provide accessor methods where necessary.

This is a general principle and you should bear in mind that *not* all instance variables are candidates for accessor methods. For example, if we had provided a getBankAccount() accessor method in the Customer class, we would be introducing the dependency between Customer and its clients that we discussed earlier.

Since the introduction of Java Beans in JDK 1.1 we also have a naming strategy which allows us to make the names of the accessor methods consistent, improving predictability and readability.

Sun refer to the use of getFieldName() and setFieldName() methods as a pattern but we do not think of it as a pattern in the class design context, so we have chosen to call it a naming strategy to avoid confusion.

So for the point class the following would be preferable:

```
private int x_;
private int y_;
public int getX()        { return x_; }
public void setX(int x)  { x_ = x; }
public int getY()        { return y_; }
public void setY(int y)  { y_ = y; }
```

Not only does this decouple the class from the classes that use it, but also it prepares the class to become a Beans-based plug and play component, because the introspection and reflection elements of Java can work on the class at runtime.

Earlier we mentioned that the rationale for the Point class having public instance variables would most likely have been due to performance issues and that it is possible to have an efficient and encapsulated class – here is how to do it:

```
final public int getX()   { return x_;}
```

So what is going on here?

By using the final modifier, we are telling the compiler that it can accelerate the use of this method by stating directly that this method cannot be overridden by another class.

This allows the compiler to "inline" the method so you get the best of both worlds – performance and encapsulation.

Please note the careful usage of the word "allows" in that last sentence – not all Java compilers do this or indeed should do this! While we are on the subject, all private methods are considered final in Java – you cannot override them and you get the benefit of "inlining" for free – this time most compilers do perform this optimization, also all methods in a class declared as final are considered final.

When a compiler "inlines" a method it inserts the method body at the location of the method call. For example, if we write the code

```
Point p = new Point(10,10);
int   x = p.getX();
```

an optimizing compiler can generate code for the assignment to the int x that is equivalent to int x=p.x_, that is, if getX() is declared final or class Point is declared final.

P Make accessor methods for instance variables "final."

The underlying reason that we make this a general principle is that accessor methods are so closely tied to the instance field that they set or get, that we can consider them as a unit. If you encounter a situation where you feel an accessor method to an instance variable should not be declared final it is worth reconsidering your design. Frequently this indicates that the method should be declared as abstract in a superclass.

Hopefully by now we will have convinced you that making instance variable private is a good thing, but what about the protected and package access modifiers?

The protected keyword allows default access within a package, sometimes referred to as "friendly," but also allows subclasses declared in other packages access to the protected method or instance variable.

Some texts suggest using the protected keyword so that the subclass (or extending class) can get to the members of the class being extended. However, all of the same encapsulation arguments still apply. If the use of the term extended is confusing here, do not worry, it is explained in the next chapter. By not going through the public interface of a class we make inheriting classes dependent on the parent class. This is fine if we have got the inheritance structure right first time (an assumption we never make), but locks us in, in exactly the same way as class dependency in any other form if we need to change things later. So be careful; protected or "friendly" access is tantamount to using public access, at least within an unstructured or non-package-based system.

P Only use protected instance variables or protected constructors in well-defined packages.

In fact some people, including Gamma *et al.*, comment that in general inheritance breaks encapsulation, as subclasses have access to the inner working of their super-class. These are complex issues that need to be explored in greater depth than there is room for here, but we will discuss this further in the next chapter on inheritance.

Oh, and just for completeness, we always explicitly state the access modifier for every instance variable to avoid the use of the default "package" scope. We also make the access modifier the first modifier to be applied in any modifier list.

Extending encapsulated systems

So back to encapsulation and some more code. This is a system that is being built for a supermarket customer recording system. Below is a very simple Customer class that simply contains the customer's name and a customer reference number that uniquely identifies the customer. This class also is on its way to becoming a well-behaved

Bean through the use of the naming strategy for its accessor methods that we described.

```
public class Customer
{
  private String name_ = ""; //for clarity
  private String refNumber_ = "";

  public Customer() {}
  public Customer(String name, String refNumber)
  {
    name_ = name;
    refNumber_ = refNumber;
  }
  public String getName()
  { return name_;}
  public String getReferenceNumber()
  { return refNumber_ ;}
  public void setName(String name)
  { name_=name; }
  public void setReferenceNumber(String refNumber)
  { refNumber_ = refNumber; }
}
```

This has been built into our new customer system in order to be able to find the customer's name from the number that appears on their swipe card. However, following a short period of user testing we came across a real problem. As the number of customers grew, the time to look up the customer's information was growing, along with the amount of information stored in the database.

In the original design we had given each of the customers an eight-digit number with leading zeros that was stored in a String. We had introduced a degree of flexibility here in case we needed to introduce other non-numeric characters into the customer reference later. As it turned out, a limitation of the swipe card and card reader meant that we could only ever store eight-digit numbers, and so we were limited by "external" design forces.

Now, we knew that we could change the internal storage of the reference number to an integer which occupies four bytes, instead of at least 16 bytes stored in an eight-digit representation of a number in a String. Remember that in Java each character is two bytes long. More importantly, we could directly access each customer's name and details by using the int as a key rather than the String version which requires either numeric conversions or hashing, in order to find entries in our storage system, which greatly accelerated the performance of the system.

This left us with only one problem: we had supplied the Customer class to external project contractors who had been using the methods in the class to write a whole stack of software to work with the user interface of the system. We did not want to redesign and respecify this code to the contractors and take the extra expense of them rewriting their code.

However, because we had forced the contractors, the clients of the class, to use the `public` methods of the class via the accessor methods, it was possible to change the internals of the `Customer` class without the contractors having to rewrite all of the code that was accessing the customer reference information that they had spent so long developing.

So instead of storing the customer reference as a `String` we could now store it as an `int`, without impacting the delivery schedule or cost of our project. Here is the new version of the customer class:

```java
public class Customer
{
  private String name_ = "";
  private int refNumber_;

  public Customer() {}
  public Customer(String name, String refNumber)
    //implicitly throws NumberFormatException
  {
    name_ = name;
    setReferenceNumber( refNumber );
  }

  public Customer(String name, int refNumber)
  {
    name_ = name;
    refNumber_ = refNumber;
  }
  // get and sets for name stay the same
  public String getName()  { return name_; }
  public void setName(String name)  { name_ = name; }

  // old methods now contain converters
  public String getReferenceNumber()
  { return Integer.toString(refNumber_ ); }

  public void setReferenceNumber(String refNumber)
    //implicitly throws NumberFormatException
  {
    try
    {
      refNumber_ = Integer.parseInt(refNumber);
    }
    catch (NumberFormatException nfe)
    {
      String err="Bad Customer reference provided ";
      err+=nfe.getMessage();
      throw new NumberFormatException( err );
    }
  }
```

```
// new methods for references
public int getIntegerReferenceNumber()
{ return refNumber_;}
public void setReferenceNumber(int refNumber)
{ refNumber_ = refNumber; }
}
```

We have only changed the interface (publicly accessible items) of the Customer class by adding some new methods, and so we know that the class will work with all of the "external" software that has already been written.

A "side effect" benefit has been that we can now trap and rethrow, with a meaningful message, an exception caused by the conversion methods, to check that the external consultants' code is always providing a reference number in the correct format. So the overall quality of the system may well also increase.

You may also notice that it has been necessary to use a longer name for one of the new methods – getIntegerReferenceNumber(). This is because it is not possible to overload methods on just the return type, so although this was fine for setReferenceNumber() which has a different parameter, int as opposed to String, it was not OK to keep the same name for getReferenceNumber() because it would have clashed with the old version. This is less than perfect, but we are prepared to live with it given all of the other benefits that we have achieved.

Packages

Classes are not the only things that we can use to slice up the Java software world and manage complexity in our systems. Packages can be used to divide up the problem space into larger chunks. Packages are an extremely simple but also extremely useful feature of the Java language.

If you take a look at the packages in the Java library you will see that they are separated into "functional" groups. For instance, java.awt is the abstract windowing toolkit, and java.io deals with all of the input/output side of Java. If you are writing any non-trivial Java system we suggest that you use packages.

(P)   Use packages constantly to manage complexity.

One of the beauties of Java is that the same ideas keep popping up at different levels of abstraction in a slightly different form. We can view a package as though it were a large class. The public classes within the packages may be viewed as the external interface to this "large class," in that they are visible to the outside world. The classes with default or "package" scope can be viewed as internal to the package, like private methods in a class, and hence not visible to the "outside world."

Here is a little code from the Acme company's user interface component library:

```
package com.acme.gui;

public class AcmeUI
{
  //public methods visible outside this package
  public Component makeButton() {...}
}

class StatusBar
{
  //methods only visible in this package
  public void setText(String message) {...}
}
```

In this case the class AcmeUI is visible to the "world," whereas the StatusBar class has the default (package) visibility and can only be instantiated by other classes in the com.acme.gui package.

Again we can also use this technique to reduce the overall coupling in a system, this time at a much higher level of abstraction. Using package local classes is a great way of reducing interclass dependency at the package interface level. Or to put it another way, package local classes are not visible across package boundaries, hence their use reduces inter-package coupling.

P If a class is only used within a package, make it package local (default visibility) to reduce system-level coupling.

In the world of patterns and idioms, the use of a package with a limited number of public classes, or a single public class, to limit external coupling is called a Facade. In *Design Patterns* (Gamma *et al.*, 1995) this is described in the following way:

Provide a unified interface to a set of interfaces in a subsystem. Facade defines a higher level interface that makes the subsystem easier to use.

So, using a combination of packages and scope in Java has got us to our first Java idiom – we hope that was not too painful. Of course, we could have done this by using public and private classes rather than packages; in fact there are many variations on the Facade theme and this is one of a number of ways of expressing this pattern as a Java idiom, but using packages and access modifiers is an extremely elegant idiom in Java for implementing the Facade pattern.

Inner classes

We have said that packages scale up from classes in terms of collecting a number of classes together into a package "name space." If we scale down from classes we arrive at inner classes.

There are four types of inner classes which can be grouped into two basic forms.

The first form is nested top-level classes and interfaces. These classes exist inside another class but are visible outside this containing class. Nested interfaces are always visible outside of their containing class. To make a nested class visible outside its containing class, the keyword `static` is used to show that the class is a nested "top-level" class.

In this form the containing class is acting exactly like a package. Here is what Simon Roberts and Philip Heller say in the *Java 1.1 Certification Study Guide* (1998):

> The net result is that a static inner class is really just a top-level class with a modified naming scheme. In fact, you can use static inner classes as an extension to packaging.

So why do we need these, given that the reuse in a new context of the `static` keyword may be obfuscating to the casual reader? Given that packages already exist to manage name spaces and we have never had cause to use nested top-level classes nor seen their use in any commercially deployed Java, we adopted the following principle.

P Prefer the use of packages over static inner classes.

The other basic form of inner classes is the set of nested classes that are not visible outside of their containing class. These are member classes, local classes, and anonymous classes. For a precise definition of these classes you might like to refer to the Java language specification from Java 1.1.

This set of classes exists within other classes as "helpers." The main use of these types of classes has been to implement the event handlers that are used in the Java 1.1 event model. We have to admit that after a first flush of enthusiasm for inner classes, and an attempt to apply them in a number of areas, this has been their main use to date. This has not been helped by a number of partial compiler implementations for supporting the inner classes language specification.

Inner classes tend to be characterized by providing very specific code for the class that contains them and little or no "state" of their own. Remember that inner classes have access to their containing classes' member fields automatically. It is interesting to note that as an inner class grows to contain its own instance fields, and more general behavior to support and manipulate this inner state, it undergoes an immense design "push" to become a top-level class in its own right where it can be reused by other classes within its package, or possibly outside its package.

P An inner class only makes sense, and should only be used, if it is going to associate and be visible only to the class that contains it.

Supporters of inner classes claim that they are elegant, concise, and expressive, and point to the fact that adapter classes can be defined in the same place as the classes that use them, which avoids pollution of the package name spaces.

On the other hand, some programmers claim that inner classes impede reuse and replace pollution of the package name space with pollution and obfuscation of the class code itself, especially in the case of anonymous classes.

It appears that inner classes are very well suited to some specific applications, for example implementing event handlers for the Java 1.1 event model for the AWT and Java Beans, but have some inherent limitations in other areas of Java program design.

SUMMARY

Classes form the basic building blocks for constructing Java software. Encapsulation allows us to build systems that are more robust and tolerant to change, and these systems should also be less interdependent. The side-effect benefits of encapsulation are manifold, from increased prospects for reuse, through to better performance.

We can scale up encapsulation techniques in Java by using packages, and use the same encapsulation principles at this higher level of abstraction. The Facade pattern can be implemented as a Java idiom by using packages and access modifiers. Scaling down, we can use inner classes; again the same encapsulation principles and benefits can be applied.

If you do nothing more than follow the principles in this chapter you can expect the benefits that we have outlined, but why stop here? We are only just beginning, and when we start to use these encapsulation principles in combination with those on inheritance, developed in the next chapter, you will start to see how Java language styles and idioms develop and become extremely powerful and useful.

2 Inheritance

Inheritance for reuse

Generalization

Delegation

Implicit inheritance

Abstraction

Interfaces

Abstract classes

Final classes

Introduction

In the previous chapter we looked at how to structure classes so that they can make use of each other by invoking (calling) methods on each other, rather than accessing their internal instance fields directly. In general terms you can think of this relationship as "*uses*" – one class uses another class. However, in OO modeling languages the term "*uses*" has a more specific meaning, with different terminology to describe other types of relationship between classes, such as association and aggregation. These are mentioned in the UML summary.

Those people starting to use Java who come from a functional or modular-based programming background may well have come across some of the ideas in Chapter 1 in one form or another. However, because Java is an object-oriented language we can also define and use another type of relationship, namely inheritance.

The whole topic of inheritance and its many facets is vast, and it would warrant a complete book on this single subject alone. So in this chapter we will be concentrating on introducing the main principles of inheritance and how to implement them in the Java language. As you progress through this book we hope to show you how inheritance and encapsulation are two of the driving forces behind most of the idioms and patterns presented.

Although the language mechanisms for implementing inheritance are the same in most languages, inheritance is used in a number of ways for different purposes in various idioms and patterns. In this chapter we examine a number of these different forms of inheritance, including inheritance for reuse and inheritance for generalization.

Java is one of the first languages to offer separate keywords to differentiate between various forms of inheritance. The most interesting of these is the use of interfaces. From a design and idioms point of view, interfaces are the single most powerful feature of Java. Interfaces are used consistently in well-designed object-oriented Java software, and form an essential part of distributed object systems. But more of interfaces later; for the moment, let us start our journey through this topic by looking at some basic uses of the inheritance mechanism.

Inheritance for reuse

The first form of inheritance that we are going to consider is using inheritance to extend the roles and responsibilities of classes that already exist.

For an example of inheritance for reuse we are going to take a look at a system that we were developing when Java 1.0 had just been released. One of the system's requirements was the ability to store and manage dates. It was also necessary to be able to work out the date for tomorrow and yesterday for any given date.

A review of the java.util.Date class showed us that this class had all of the features that we were looking for apart from the ability to work out the date for tomorrow and yesterday. In this case it did not make sense to create a completely new Date class from scratch and so we decided to "extend" the Date class from the Java library by adding the features that we required. This class was called ExtendedDate. Here is the code:

```java
public class ExtendedDate
  extends java.util.Date
{
  public void incDay(int numberOfDaysForward)
  {
    //..move this date numberOfDaysForward
  }
  public void decDay(int numberOfDaysBackward)
  {
    //..move this date numberOfDaysBackward
  }
}
```

You will see that the methods that we finally supplied went further than the original specification. This was because we thought that the system would also need to work out the date in a week's time, or any arbitrary number of days in the future or past. To solve this you will see that we made the increment or decrement methods take an integer parameter that represented how many days to wind the date forward or backward.

So now when we have an instance of ExtendedDate we can increment or decrement these instances by arbitrary amounts but still also use all of the methods of the java.util.Date class. Here is some example code, using the extending methods in ExtendedDate and some of the methods from the java.util.Date class, via the instances of the ExtendedDate class.

```
ExtendedDate date = new ExtendedDate();
date.incDay(1);  //tomorrow's date
int dayOfMonth = date.getDate();  //from Date (JDK 1.0)
int monthNumber = date.getMonth();  //from Date

System.out.println("Tomorrow will be day "+ dayOfMonth +
    " of month " + monthNumber);

// or for yesterday
ExtendedDate date = new ExtendedDate();
date.decDay(1);

// or this day next week
ExtendedDate date = new ExtendedDate();
date.incDay(7);
```

This looks fine but although we said that all of the methods of the java.util.Date class are also available in the ExtendedDate class this is not wholly true. We have to keep in mind the following Java rule when we use the extends keyword to implement inheritance.

(R)   Constructors are not inherited.

So if we try this:

```
ExtendedDate specificDate = new ExtendedDate(89, 8, 15);
```

in order to make a specific date instance for our ExtendedDate, the compiler will tell us that there is no constructor available for ExtendedDate with that number of parameters, even though we know that there is a constructor of this type in the java.util.Date class. We therefore need to write a set of constructors that call the constructors in the java.util.Date class that we are extending from.

```
public class java.util.Date extends java.util.Date
{
  public ExtendedDate() //default constructor
  {
    super();
  }
  public ExtendedDate(int year, int month, int day)
  {
    super(year, month, day);
  }
  //etc. for all of java.util.Date constructors

  // now the new methods for incDay and decDay
}
```

You will see that it is necessary to define the default constructor as well in the above code, because the compiler will no longer generate the default constructor code "secretly," owing to the fact that we have defined other constructors. We have made use of super here as well. In this case super is used as a superclass constructor method call (that is, in the form where it is followed by round brackets) in order to call the constructor of the class that is being extended. We call this class the parent or "superclass" of the inheriting class, hence the use of the keyword super.

Now that we have had to define all of these constructors, our "free" use of the underlying java.util.Date class is looking a little less appealing than our initial version.

In fact we have introduced a strong dependency (coupling) between the constructors of the super java.util.Date class and the extending ExtendedDate class. For example, if there is a change to any of the constructors in the superclass this must be reflected in the code for the subclass (ExtendedDate). This is exactly the type of problem we were trying to avoid in the previous chapter and indeed throughout this book.

So be very careful with inheritance for reuse; it is one of those techniques that is extremely appealing because it offers very powerful and simple ways to add features to your software at apparently little cost, but it also carries a number of downsides. If you are looking at some code and you find deep inheritance hierarchies, you may find that inheritance for reuse is the culprit that is making the code hard to understand, slow, and occupy far too much memory.

(P) Keep inheritance hierarchies small.

As a very general rule of thumb, keep an eye on any hierarchy that grows beyond five levels of extensions, and check carefully to make sure that inheritance for reuse is not causing some of these problems.

There are a number of ways of implementing reuse without using inheritance. As it transpired in the example above, later in the project we got rid of the ExtendedDate class and defined a utility class (a class containing only static methods) that could increment and decrement dates that were supplied to it, to get over just these types of problems.

Another way to get round this problem is to use delegation. That is, define a class to do the extra work we need and then use that class from within a calling class, hence delegating the work onto the new class. More on delegation later but for the moment:

(P) Prefer delegation or using utility classes over inheritance for reuse.

Sometimes inheritance for reuse is referred to as a weak form of inheritance, for some of the reasons we have outlined. So be careful with inheritance for reuse. Now let us move on to look at a use of the extends keyword to achieve another form of inheritance.

Generalization
....

In order to understand the process of generalization, let us take a look at an example from a lightweight user interface component library for Java. One of the components to be defined in this library is a Scrollbar. At each end of the Scrollbar there are going to be boxes that the user can press to make Scrollbar's "thumb," the icon in the middle of the bar, move towards the box that the user is pressing.

Our initial design has shown that we are going to need four types of Boxes – UpBox, DownBox, LeftBox, and RightBox. These will contain arrows pointing in the direction appropriate for each box.

Here is some very simplified code that we wrote as an initial test for our class design. First the UpBox class. Unfortunately, in these examples we have to access the public fields of Rectangle directly because the class does not provide any accessor methods.

```java
public class UpBox
{
  public static final int ARROW_SIZE = 5;
  private Rectangle bounds_ = null;


  public UpBox(Rectangle boundingRectangle)
  {
    bounds_ = boundingRectangle;
  }
  public void paint(Graphics g)
  {
    // draw the box background and beveled 3d border
    g.setColor(Color.gray);
    g.fillRect(bounds_.x, bounds_.y,
      bounds_.width, bounds_.height);
    g.draw3DRect(bounds_.x, bounds_.y,
      bounds_.width-1,bounds_.height-1, false);


    // set the color and find the center of the box
    g.setColor(Color.black);
    int x = bounds_.x + ( bounds_.width/2 );
    int y = bounds_.y + ( bounds_.height/2 );


    // move y to the top of the arrow and scan down
    y -= (ARROW_SIZE/2);
    for (int scan = 0; scan < ARROW_SIZE; scan++)
      g.drawLine(x+scan, y+scan, x-scan, y+scan);
  }
}
```

When the `paint` method is called on the `UpBox` it will use the `Graphics` object g that is supplied as a parameter, in order to draw the box and the up arrow. Now let us do the same for the `DownBox` class.

```
public class DownBox
{
  public static final int ARROW_SIZE = 5;
  private Rectangle bounds_ = null;

  public DownBox(Rectangle boundingRectangle)
  {
    bounds_ = boundingRectangle;
  }
  public void paint(Graphics g)
  {
    // draw the box background and beveled 3d border
    g.setColor(Color.gray);
    g.fillRect(bounds_.x,bounds_.y,
        bounds_.width,bounds_.height);
    g.draw3DRect(bounds_.x,bounds_.y,
        bounds_.width,bounds_.height-1, false);

    // set the color and find the center of the box
    g.setColor(Color.black);
    int x = bounds_.x + ( bounds_.width/2 );
    int y = bounds_.y + ( bounds_.height/2 );

    // move y to the bottom of the arrow and scan up
    y += (ARROW_SIZE/2);
    for (int scan = 0; scan < ARROW_SIZE; scan++)
        g.drawLine(x+scan, y-scan, x-scan, y-scan);

  }
}
```

If you are thinking, "Hang on a second, it looks like you've just copied and pasted most of the code from `UpBox`," you are on the right track!

There is more code here that is general to both classes than there is code that is specific to each. It is definitely time for review because it seems that going on to write `LeftBox` and `RightBox` will result in even more unnecessary duplication.

Another thing that you may notice about both of these classes is that we are directly accessing the members of the `Rectangle` class because this class does not offer final gets and sets for our use. This goes against an earlier design principle and so we are also going to make it a goal, as we evolve the code, to localize these accesses to reduce their impact.

What we can do is move the commonly repeated code up into a superclass that each of the specific boxes can inherit from in order to do the general work, leaving them simply to implement their own special behavior. This process of migrating or "factoring out" common fields and behavior is known as generalization.

Here is the generalized Box superclass:

```
class Box
{
  public static final int ARROW_SIZE = 5;
  private Rectangle bounds_ = null;

  public Box(Rectangle boundingRectangle)
  {
    bounds_ = boundingRectangle;
  }
  public final int getCenterX()
  {
    return bounds_.x + ( bounds_.width/2 );
  }
  public final int getCenterY()
  {
    return bounds_.y + ( bounds_.height/2 );
  }
  public void paint(Graphics g)
  {
    // draw the box background and beveled 3d border
    g.setColor(Color.gray);
    g.fillRect(bounds_.x, bounds_.y,
        bounds_.width, bounds_.height);
    g.draw3DRect(bounds_.x, bounds_.y,
        bounds_.width-1,bounds_.height-1, false);
  }
}
```

Now the Box superclass is doing just about all of the general work, leaving us with a greatly shrunk set of classes which inherit from it. Here is the UpBox rewritten to use the generalized Box class:

```
public class UpBox extends Box
{
  public UpBox(Rectangle boundingRectangle)
  {
    super(boundingRectangle); // just pass the rectangle up
  }
  public void paint(Graphics g)
  {
    // draw the general box backgound
    super.paint(g);

    // draw the up arrow
    g.setColor(Color.black);
    int x = getCenterX(); //inherited from Box
```

```
    int y = getCenterY() - (Box.ARROW_SIZE/2);
    for (int scan = 0; scan < Box.ARROW_SIZE; scan++)
        g.drawLine(x+scan, y+scan, x-scan, y+scan);
  }
}
```

Our code for the four child `Box` classes has been greatly reduced and also the instance variable for the `Rectangle` class has not been repeated in each of the child classes. This has allowed us to eliminate any reference to its instance fields in the four child classes. In accord with our earlier principles on encapsulation we have made `final` accessor methods to return the center coordinates of the box and denied direct access to the `Rectangle` class.

Overall, by isolating the responsibilities for various parts of the task to well-defined classes, and by applying generalization and encapsulation principles, we have made the code easier to write, and more importantly far easier to maintain.

Performing generalizations such as this often happens as part of the iterative cycle of object-oriented software development. Having tried out the design by writing some code, we have evolved the design. This means that it is necessary to check the design again to make sure that the overall model of the software is still valid. One of the tasks of developing an object-oriented system is to continually balance what makes sense in terms of the system's design with what can be practical and useful in terms of actually writing code. This is a driving force behind using an iterative software process with built-in checks to ensure that the design of the system stays coherent.

It is possible to do a simple check to see if inheritance is valid in a particular case. In the case of the Scrollbar Box example it is possible to say that an UpBox is a type of Box. Whenever we come across the words *"is a type of"* we know that we have a candidate for inheritance. In fact, it is a good principle to apply the *"is a type of"* question to all inheritance relationships.

(P)   Inheritance is a class-based, "is a type of" relationship.

Please remember that this is a general principle. The English language can twist and turn on us in many strange ways, and so this principle may not always apply, but in general terms it is good way of sniffing out and checking inheritance relationships. One caveat: do not get confused between *"is a type of"* and *"is an instance of."* This is a common problem that people encounter when they first start to use inheritance, because it is quite often very hard to make this "call." If in doubt seek out your local "guru" for some classification advice.

Delegation

Earlier on we mentioned that another way to address factoring out common code and storage was to delegate some of the work to another object that can do some of the general work for us. Using the `Box` example we could convert the code for the client Boxes to use delegation instead of generalized inheritance.

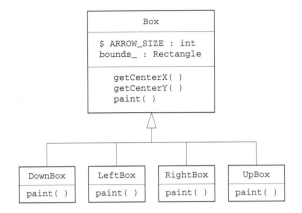

Figure 2.1 Box example using inheritance

Figure 2.1 shows the UML diagram for the generalized example.

Here is the DownBox delegating its common behavior and storage to an instance of a Box class:

```
public class DownBox
{
  private Box box_;

  public DownBox(Rectangle boundingRectangle)
  {
    box_ = new Box(boundingRectangle);
  }

  public void paint(Graphics g)
  {
    // draw the general box background
    box_.paint(g);

    // draw the down arrow
    g.setColor(Color.black);
    int x = box_.getCenterX();
    int y = box_.getCenterY() + (Box.ARROW_SIZE/2);

    for (int scan = 0; scan < Box.ARROW_SIZE; scan++)
        g.drawLine(x+scan, y-scan, x-scan, y-scan);
  }
}
```

Using delegation, the UML diagram looks as shown in Figure 2.2.

As you can see, the inheriting and delegating versions of the set of Box classes look extremely similar. There were no changes to the Box class, and the various client box classes simply make an instance of the Box class which they then reference rather than using super to reference the methods that they require.

Figure 2.2 DownBox example using delegation

In some cases delegation can be a better form of generalization than inheritance, especially when classes that use another class can share the class being used. This has both performance and memory advantages over inheritance-based generalization. However, in some cases inheritance allows us to be more sophisticated in our designs and also enables polymorphism which delegation is not designed to cope with.

Implicit inheritance

Given the inheriting version of the UpBox class that we were using earlier:

```
public class UpBox extends Box
{
  public UpBox (Rectangle boundingRectangle)
  {
    super (boundingRectangle);
  }
  public void paint (Graphics g)
  {
    // code for paint
  }
}
```

it is possible to write the following legal code as a client of the UpBox class:

```
UpBox upBox = new UpBox (new Rectangle (10,10,10,10) );
String boxString = upBox.toString();
```

So where has the method toString() appeared from? It is not in UpBox and it is not in Box, but it is in the class Object.

What the compiler has "secretly" done is make the Box class extend the class Object. So the line

```
public class Box
```

could be read, or indeed written, more explicitly as:

```
public class Box extends Object
```

All classes implicitly extend the class `Object`.

This has some quite profound implications, in that all classes either directly or indirectly inherit from the class `Object`. For instance, casting any class to the class `Object` is always going to be legal, although in the following example, totally unnecessary:

```
UpBox upBox= new UpBox(new Rectangle(10,10,10,10) );

Object obj= (Object) upBox;    //don't need cast
obj.toString();
```

This means that all of the methods in `java.lang.Object` are always available to any object. We are going to come back to the ability to assign any object that you create or use to the type `Object` later on, when we consider collections and other generic code forms towards the end of the book.

In the code comment above we mentioned that the cast to the type `Object` is unnecessary. This is because all objects and array instances are implicitly of the type `Object`. This leads us to another general principle:

Avoid unnecessary casting.

We make this a general principle not only from a correctness standpoint, but also from a performance one. Consider the unnecessary cast below:

```
LeftBox leftBox = new LeftBox(new Rectangle(10,10,10,10));
Box box = (Box)leftBox;
int midX = box.getCenterX();
int midY = box.getCenterY();
```

Casts are generally an expensive operation because they involve checking the class information at runtime, but the important aspect here is to understand that any subclass (extending class) is implicitly the same type as its superclass – remember the "*is a type of*" test – and so any methods, that are available through their access specifiers, defined on superclasses are available directly to a reference of any subtype. So in the above case the `LeftBox` reference may be used to directly access the "get" methods declared in the `Box` class.

```
LeftBox leftBox = new LeftBox(new Rectangle(10,10,10,10));
int midX = leftBox.getCenterX();
int midY = leftBox.getCenterY();
```

This code compiles and works fine, as well as being simpler and working faster than the previous example.

Abstraction

You may have come across the term abstraction being used with respect to discussions on inheritance. In fact we can say that all of the classes in our system are abstractions of the "real world model" that we are constructing in software.

We have already seen how to build a number of relationships between objects, and how to establish *"is a type of"* inheritance relationships between classes. Generally in an object-oriented design, when we talk about abstraction, we are referring to the class-based model (or classification) of the problem space.

Given that a good class model is key to building any object-oriented system, the design skill of abstracting out the essential elements and features of classes is key to the underlying strength of our object-oriented system. Or to put it another way, we could say that our class hierarchy has to be well founded so that it can tolerate change.

Up to this point we have just been using "vanilla" Java classes to build inheritance and *uses* relationships. However, there are two forms that help us to be more precise and expressive with our use of abstractions to solve programming problems in the Java world, namely interfaces and abstract classes.

Interfaces

From a design point of view an interface is, in essence, a guarantee that any class that implements it will contain the Java code to implement all of the methods listed in that interface. In fact, if you write an implementing class that is not abstract and does not define method bodies for all of the methods in the interface, the compiler will keep telling you about it until you do. Look kindly on the compiler because we can turn this pedantry to our advantage by making the compiler spot errors at compile time rather than at runtime when they are generally much harder to find and fix, and are likely to impact users.

Interfaces can define method signatures and static final fields only. Sometimes these method signatures alone are called operations, and static final fields are also termed named constants. The key point to interfaces is that it is simply not possible to define the implementation of any methods within the interface, that is, an interface can only outline the intended behavior for a set of methods.

Here is an example of a simple interface for any type of device that plays audio signals. Although we have explicitly declared the method signatures as public in all interfaces, these methods are implicitly public abstract, whereas fields are implicitly public static final.

```
public interface AudioPlayer
{
  public void play();
  public void stop();
  public void pause();
  public void skipForward();
  public void skipBackwards();
}
```

This is a list of the operations that any class that wants to conform to this interface (guarantee) must define in order to say that it implements this interface. We often refer to a class that implements *all* the methods defined in an interface such as this as a *concrete class*. Interfaces are not "concrete" because we can never make instances of them by using the new keyword. The code

```
AudioPlayer audioInterface = new AudioPlayer(); //illegal
```

will produce a compiler error. For this reason it does not make any sense for an interface to define any constructors; this would be pointless because we already know that constructors cannot be inherited and anyway we could not define any behavior in them even if they were.

Interfaces cannot define constructors.

So if we cannot define constructors for an interface it is always necessary to make concrete classes that implement them in order to make use of them. In this example a mini disc player is our concrete class:

```
public class MiniDiscPlayer
   implements AudioPlayer
{
   // constructors
   // implement all of the operations defined in the interface
   public void play()
   {/* code to implement play method */}

   public void stop()
   {/* code to implement stop method */}

   // etc. for all of the AudioPlayer operations

   // these methods are specific to a mini disc player
   void loadNewDisc(MiniDisc md)
   {/* code to load a new disc */}
}
```

It is easy see how other classes such as CD players, tape players, and hard disk recorders can also implement this interface, although the underlying implementation and storage model would be totally different. If we are lucky and have done our homework well enough we might be able to map this interface onto new types of audio devices that have not been invented yet, giving us a high degree of "future proofing."

If all of the classes that reproduce audio within our system implement this interface, and hence guarantee that they will produce the appropriate behavior when these operations are invoked, then we can happily write client software against this guarantee without worrying about the details of the underlying implementation. For example, if we were to substitute a CD player for our mini disc player, we would expect all of the client code written to the AudioPlayer interface to still work as expected without any changes. This is wonderful from a robustness point of view because it means that we can make changes to the implementation behind the interface without them echoing out, like ripples on water, through all of the code that we have already written in our clients of the interface. This really helps us to build robust systems that can tolerate changes and additions without breaking the basic structure of our code.

Interfaces enable us to make this benefit real by providing the ability to split the code that uses a class interface, the client code, from the implementation of the class, as we discussed in Chapter 1. As a programmer it is always important to support this by writing code that uses the interface of a class and that does not depend on the internal structure, or indeed specific methods of a class, when general ones would equally apply.

P Program to an interface, not to an implementation.

Those people interested in pursing the ideas of decoupling the interface from the implementation of classes may like to look at the Bridge pattern in *Design Patterns* (Gamma *et al.*, 1995). Other references to this type of pattern may use the term handle/body. The basis of this pattern is to be able to have a reference to an interface that may be implemented by one or more concrete classes.

Abstract classes

Some classes are really useful as classes that we can inherit from as we have seen in the generalization example, but sometimes these classes do not really make any sense in terms of objects existing in the context of the client code. As an example, while we are writing this book there is an exhibition being staged at the Natural History Museum in Kensington, London, entitled Mammals.

We know some of the properties of a mammal and some of the expected behaviors of a mammal, so it is a pretty safe assumption that this is going to be a useful abstraction. As a case in point we can make a decision on whether or not to attend the exhibition based on our interest in mammals. For these reasons we know that there must be some real substance in the concept of a mammal.

If we were to go to the exhibition, we might be interested in monkeys and go along to the Monkey section or go to the Panda section to find out more about pandas, but we would not expect to go to the mammal section and find a stuffed mammal! That is, a mammal is a classification, not a living species.

If we were asked to come up with a class model of this situation, we have a very interesting problem; we want to be able to define a class of type Mammal, and define some of the properties and behaviors of that class because we know that this is going to be really useful, but it does not make sense to actually make an object from that class; it only makes sense to inherit from that class.

P If a class is designed to be inherited, but it does not make sense to have an instance of the class, it should be defined as abstract.

In this case we use the keyword abstract to state that the class cannot be instantiated (made into an object) by the Java environment. In fact if we apply the new operator to an abstract class the compiler will produce an error.

```
abstract class AbstractMammal
{
  //these methods must be implemented by a subclass
  public abstract void walk();
  public abstract void eat();
}
```

Methods declared within an abstract class that do not have a method body must be also be declared as abstract and implemented by a subclass – hang on, isn't that the same as a Java interface?

Yes, in this context, so what is the difference between an abstract class and an interface?

An abstract class declared with method signatures only (no method body) and static final fields (constants) is effectively the same as an interface; however, you have to "extend" an abstract class, not implement it. As you know, a subclass can only extend a single superclass, but can implement many interfaces. So as a general principle you should change abstract classes that only contain method signatures and named constants into interfaces – this reinforces the principle "Program to an interface, not to an implementation."

> **P** Abstract classes that contain only method signatures and static final fields should be declared as interfaces.

There is more to abstract classes than just declaring method signatures. An abstract class can contain fields, class variables (statics), method signatures, and fully implemented methods as well.

For example, a cut-down version of our abstract Mammal class could be declared as follows:

```
abstract class AbstractMammal
{
  private int gestation_;  //gestation period
  //other fields

  public final int getGestationPeriod()
  {
    return gestation_;
  }

  //method signatures, these must be implemented by a subclass
  public abstract void walk();
  public abstract void eat();
}
```

An abstract class's usefulness is realized when you perform generalization, migrating common state in the form of fields, and behavior in the form of methods, to a superclass. We used generalization in our Scrollbar Box example earlier in the chapter. In that example, drawing a Box without an arrow in it was also a useful and meaningful thing to do and so it was implemented as a concrete class. However, in these examples we were simply introducing the concept of inheritance; there is another form of inheritance, namely *specialization*, that we are going to discuss in the next chapter, which can be an exceptionally powerful use of abstract classes, but for the moment let us round out this chapter by discussing `final` classes.

Final classes

Just before we summarize this chapter it is interesting to introduce a counter point to abstract classes. In some cases it is necessary to state that a class is specifically not to be inherited from, or to put it another way, the class must be a leaf or node in the class hierarchy. In these cases use the modifier `final` before declaring the class, to show that no other classes can inherit from it.

```
public final class YouCantInheritThis
{
    // class internals
}
```

There are a number of cases where Java software benefits from the ability of classes to inhibit their inheritance into other classes. If you would like to see an example, we describe an idiom called *typesafe constant* in Chapter 4, which illustrates the use of a `final` class.

From an inheritance perspective you could say that `abstract` and `final` classes are direct opposites. For this reason, if you define a class as both `abstract` and `final` the compiler will produce a terse error message leaving you in no doubt that this is a pretty dumb thing to do!

SUMMARY

Inheritance is a class-based, "*is a type of*" relationship providing a mechanism to model both natural and conceptual classifications of objects. This allows us to explicitly take advantage of the common parts and behaviors within these classifications, and to model behavior in more complete ways than is possible in non-object-oriented systems.

In Java, interfaces and abstract classes allow programmers to be more explicit about their intentions of using a particular form of inheritance. This leads to clearer expressions of patterns into language-based idioms. From a language design perspective the clear separation of interfaces away from the normal class syntax is a measure of their importance in the object-oriented world of Java.

The act of turning a design into Java code may well evolve the design. This is a motivating force in using an iterative development cycle. It is necessary to perform checks when a cycle has occurred to ensure that the design remains coherent. Design tools can help in this process by visualizing class structures and interactions as diagrams.

3 Polymorphism

What is polymorphism?

Applying polymorphism

Multiple levels of polymorphism

Introduction

In this chapter, which is the last of the introductory chapters covering the basic building blocks of OO idioms in Java, we will be adding a knowledge of polymorphism and giving examples of its use in Java systems.

What is polymorphism?

If we literally translate polymorphism, it means "taking many forms." However, as in most translations, this does not give us the full picture. We have already seen in the previous chapter how to design class hierarchies by factoring out common behavior and instance fields through the use of interface, and abstract and final classes. We also saw that a child class *is a type of* parent class.

We can say that a child class is a "specialization" of its parent class. In other words the child class can do all the things that the parent class can do, but in addition it can also do its own "special" behavior. This means that anywhere a parent class instance is expected you can also use an object of a child class in its place. In fact there is another thing that a child class can do, and that is to choose to do something that the parent class does, but in its own special way. This is the essence of polymorphism.

In order to use polymorphism we must have an inheritance hierarchy. Here is an example of a simple inheritance structure for a zoo application. In this case the Animal class is acting as the parent class and the Bear class is the child.

```
package zoo;

class Animal
{
  public void snore()
```

```
    {
       System.out.println("Animal is snoring.");
    }
    public void sleep()
    {
       System.out.println("Animal is sleeping.");
       snore();
    }
}

class Bear extends Animal
{
    //this method overrides the snore method in the Animal
    public void snore()
    {
       System.out.println("Bear is snoring.");
    }
}
```

A statement such as `Animal animal = new Bear();` is a valid Java statement because a reference to a `Bear` is also a reference to an `Animal`. This is true anywhere a parent class reference is used, whether it be a local variable, class instance variable, or a method parameter. Here is the code for a method `polyTest()` that calls the class methods defined above:

```
public void polyTest(Animal a)
{
    a.snore();
    a.sleep();
}
```

The code below shows an instance of `Bear` being passed to the `polyTest` method which takes an instance of an `Animal` as a parameter.

```
Bear  bear = new Bear();
polyTest( bear );   // fine because Bear extends Animal
```

Before we go on to examine the output of the `polyTest` method it is vital to keep in mind that it is the real type of the instantiated object that we created with the `new` keyword that is being used to determine which methods are called when methods are overridden in a class hierarchy. Just to make this distinction very clear, we use the term "real type" to mean the actual type of the class as made with `new`, and the term "apparent type" of the object to mean the type of the reference to the object.

In the case of our Bear example the following code:

```
Bear bear = new Bear();
System.out.println(bear.getClass().getName());
Animal animal = bear;
System.out.println(animal.getClass().getName());
```

```
Object obj = animal;
System.out.println(obj.getClass().getName());
```

will produce the following output:

```
zoo.Bear
zoo.Bear
zoo.Bear
```

So in this example the real type of the object is always zoo.Bear, no matter what the apparent type of the object seems to be. This means that the Java runtime can work out what the real type of any object is, no matter what the apparent type of the object is, in any context.

Now that the distinction between real and apparent type is clear, we can move on to analyze the output from the call to the polyTest() method.

```
Bear is snoring.
Animal is sleeping.
Bear is snoring.
```

Let us first examine why Bear.snore() was the first and last method to be called in the output from the sample code. From the Bear's class code we can see that Bear overrides the snore() method, and the object passed into the method polyTest() is of real type Bear, although we have passed it as the apparent type Animal.

The Java environment will first do a lookup to find the real type of the object passed as the Animal parameter. Given the real type of the object, it is then possible to find out if it has a method with a method signature that matches that of the snore() method. In this case, Bear does have a snore() method and so the Java runtime environment executes the snore() method in Bear and not in Animal.

You can do this lookup yourself by using the Java Class class and the java.lang.reflect package. This package allows you to examine all kinds of information about the type of any object. So, should you want to, by using the appropriate methods you can "hand craft" code that can implement this method lookup behavior. You may want to do this out of interest but we suggest that you may find implementing a full-blown polymorphic system in this way a little tricky and extremely slow.

Now back to our Bear example. In the case of the second call to the sleep() method, the same rules apply. The real type of the object passed into the polyTest() method is Bear, and so the Java runtime will do a lookup and find that Bear does not have a match for the sleep() method and so the Java runtime tries to find a match for the method in the Bear's parent class. The parent class is Animal and so once again the runtime tries to find a method that matches the sleep() method, hence Animal.sleep() gets called. This outputs Animal is sleeping and then invokes the snore() method.

However, when snore() is invoked in Animal, the search for the method to call starts again from the real type Bear, and so Bear.snore() will be called, not Animal.snore(), which outputs the final Bear is snoring message.

That is a "mechanical" description of polymorphic behavior and although it is important to understand and be able to predict the Java runtime behavior with respect to overridden methods, it is not necessary to understand how the environment implements this behavior. In fact it is quite possible that the Java Virtual Machine (JVM) will not use the techniques in the way that we have described to locate the correct method to call. Any way of implementing polymorphic behavior is fine so long as the apparent behavior is the same as that of the JVM standard.

Another way to think about this is to go back to the example of the video camera, the very first example in the book. If you press the video camera's Record button, the camera will record some video footage for you. It does not matter whether you call the camera a video camera, a video recording device, or just an object. It is a video camera and it will do the job that you have requested.

Whichever way you look at it, what is really important is to remember that it is the real type of the object that determines the methods that are called in any class hierarchy. The ability of the JVM to determine which method to call at runtime is called dynamic binding.

> The JVM will always search up the inheritance hierarchy from the real class of the target object, in order to find the first match for the signature of the target method, no matter what the apparent type of the object is at the time of the call.

If you come from a non-Java or non-OO background, this type of runtime behavior can cause the odd shock until you get used to this way of thinking. It is also worth noting that field access such as `public static` is based on the apparent type and not the real type of the object. As we encourage the use of accessor methods for private fields and only use non-polymorphic `public final static` fields, the apparent type is always either encapsulated or the same as the real type in our examples.

Applying polymorphism

After that brief excursion into the behavior of the Java environment it is now time to apply our newly acquired skill with polymorphism.

To understand the power of polymorphism, especially when it comes to extending or making additions to systems, it is worth looking at an example from a non-object-oriented programming language (OOPL) perspective first.

Using an example from a simple personnel system, we are going to extend its basic functionality to calculate annual bonuses. This calculation is based on various known factors about the employee. An analysis of the problem domain has produced the following functional specification for the annual bonus calculation.

Here is the pseudo code for the *non*-OO way of doing things:

```
if the employee is a director
   then use FatCatBonusCalculation function
else if the employee is a cleaner
   then use ExploitLowPaidWorkerCalculation function.
etc. etc.
```

If you have come to Java from a non-OO background then you will be all too familiar with the type of function that these requirements produce. In general the program consists of a large `switch` statement or a series of `if`, `else if` clauses to determine the type of function to call, based on a set of parameters. There are techniques you can use in some of the more powerful non-OOPLs to remove the "switching," but this book is about Java and the OO way of doing things so let us now examine how we might implement the above in Java.

In the previous chapter we introduced Java interfaces and said that "interfaces are the single most powerful feature of Java" – hopefully you will begin to see why!

One of the rules introduced in Chapter 2 was "Program to an interface, not to an implementation," hence:

```
public interface Employee
{
  public String getName();
  public float getSalary();
  public float calcAnnualBonus();
  public int getDaysOffSick();
}
```

Having defined the interface to an `Employee` hierarchy we now want to apply two of the ideas that we saw in the previous chapter.

We are going to design a class that contains common instance variables and concrete methods that we know that child classes are going to use, and we are also going to make it an abstract class because in this case it makes no sense to have a "vanilla" employee in our class model.

This happens so often in real cases that we can state it as a general rule. Remember that there may be cases where it makes sense for a parent class to be concrete rather than abstract, such as the Box example in Chapter 2, but that is the exception rather than the rule, so we can make the general principle as follows:

(P) Migrate common instance variables and concrete accessor methods to an abstract class that can lie between the interface and concrete classes in a hierarchy.

Here is the code for our abstract employee class:

```
public abstract class AbstractEmployee
  implements Employee
{
  private String name_;
  private float salary_;
  private int sickdays_;
  public AbstractEmployee(String who,float sal,int days_sick)
  {
    name_=who;
    salary_=sal;
    sickdays_= days_sick;
  }
```

```
public final String getName() {return name_;}
public float getSalary()       {return salary_;}
public int getDaysOffSick()    {return sickdays_;}
}
```

If you are wondering why we have not made the instance variable in Abstract Employee protected, now would be a good time to check back to Chapter 1.

Finally there are two concrete types of employees:

```
public final class FatCatEmployee extends AbstractEmployee
{
  public FatCatEmployee(String who,float sal,int sick_days)
  {
    super(who,sal,sick_days);
  }

  public float calcAnnualBonus()
  {
    float LoadsOfMoney=0F;
    //algorithm for fat cats
    System.out.println("FatCatEmployee.calcBonus");

    return LoadsOfMoney;
  }
}

public final class LowPaidEmployee extends AbstractEmployee
{
  public LowPaidEmployee(String who,float sal,int sick_days)
  {
    super(who,sal,sick_days);
  }

  public float calcAnnualBonus()
  {
    //algorithm for the low paid
    System.out.println("LowPaidEmployee.calcBonus");

    return 0F;
  }
}
```

Figure 3.1 shows the UML class diagram for our new class hierarchy.

You have already learnt that any instance of a subclass in a hierarchy can be assigned to a reference to its parent class or an interface that it implements. This means that we can declare a reference to an Employee, which is an interface, and assign an instance of FatCatEmployee or LowPaidEmployee to it.

```
Employee [] employee= new Employee[2];
employee[0]= new FatCatEmployee("The Boss",500000,20);
employee[1]= new LowPaidEmployee("The Tea Boy",5000,1);
```

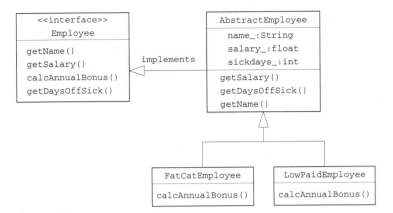

Figure 3.1 Employee hierarchy using an abstract class that contains common fields

In this example we have declared an array of Employee references and assigned instances of FatCatEmployee and LowPaidEmployee to the elements of the array. As the type of the array is Employee you can happily invoke any method declared in that interface regardless of its runtime type. This means that we can write extremely generic code to perform certain tasks on the Employee interface.

```
int num_emps=employee.length;
for(int i=0; i<num_emps;i++)
{
   employee[i].calcAnnualBonus();
}
```

And the sample code will generate the following to System.out:

```
FatCatEmployee.calcAnnualBonus()
LowPaidEmployee.calcAnnualBonus()
```

By using dynamic binding to implement polymorphism the JVM can defer the resolution of method calls to runtime where it performs a runtime lookup of the correct method to call.

Let us now focus on a more realistic and powerful example using the Employee hierarchy. In this example we have decoupled the building of a list of current employees from the functionality of iterating through them to calculate the total annual cost of all employees. For now you will just have to take our word for it that this is a wise thing to do, but we will be investigating iterators in a later chapter.

```
public final class EmployeeOperations
{
   public static float
     calcCostOfEmployees(Enumeration employees)
   {
      float total_cost=0F;
```

```
while(employees.hasMoreElements())
{
    Employee emp = (Employee)employees.nextElement();
    //emp could be an instance of any class
    //implementing Employee
    total_cost+=emp.calcAnnualBonus();
    total_cost+=emp.getSalary();
}
return total_cost;
}
}
```

The method calcCostOfEmployees() takes an Enumeration parameter so that it can be implemented independently of the actual representation of the collection class containing the objects – this may be a Vector, linked list, or Hashtable populated from a database source; the good thing here is that the EmployeeOperations class does not need to know that, nor the concrete types of Employee and, surprise, surprise, java.util.Enumeration is yet another interface!

Just as we think we have completed the enhancements to the employee system the company has decided to introduce a new class of Employee, BlueCollarEmployee. Fortunately our use of Java interfaces has protected us from this "requirements creep," leaving calcCostOfEmployees() and other methods acting solely on the unaltered interface definition – consider how difficult it is in non-OOPLs to implement a new requirement, leaving us with more "cases" in the switch statement or conditions in the if, else if clauses.

That about concludes our introduction to simple polymorphism; however, there is more to polymorphism than just lists of objects that implement an interface. So far we have examined a single level of polymorphism, sometimes referred to as "single polymorphism." Our next assignment is to delve deeper and add a second level of polymorphism.

Multiple levels of polymorphism

Nailing down system requirements is sometimes as difficult as convincing the tax inspector that your new $1000 snow board is a legitimate business expense for you in your capacity as a software developer!

Currently our employee system is suffering from just such a lack of concrete requirements. The company has now decided that they want to introduce a new pay structure which they want to be able to model in the system in order to estimate annual employment costs. They have promised us that this is the last shift in requirements – but we have heard that one before!

The crucial thing to note is that we want to be able to *model* the new pay structure indicating that runtime changes in behavior are probably required. Now you are probably thinking that this sounds like a job for polymorphism, and you would be right, but how can this be achieved when we have already constructed an inheritance hierarchy to deal with various types of employees? It is as though we need to classify the problem space in two different inheritance hierarchies so that we can use the polymorphism for both problems!

A *bad* approach to solving this problem, which sadly we see far too often in implementations, would be to pass a constant parameter into a method specifying the type of operation that is required, for example by adding static final int class variables to EmployeeOperations:

```
static final int SIMPLE_PAY_MODEL=0;
static final int INCENTIVE_PAY_MODEL=1;
```

We would then add an additional int parameter to the calcCostOfEmployees() method which specifies the type of pay model required. There are two problems with this approach. One is addressed in the next chapter on type safety and constants so we will leave that till later. The one that we are interested in here is that the method calcCostOfEmployees() would have to contain code like this:

```
if(type==SIMPLE_PAY_MODEL)
{
    //calc costs based on some known algo
}
else if(type==INCENTIVE_PAY_MODEL)
{
    //ditto
}
```

Hang on! Isn't that where we started this section, looking at how non-OOPLs implement these kinds of designs and the problems they cause?

Fortunately OOPLs like Java are flexible enough to allow us to model multiple levels of polymorphism so that we can avoid these nasty if, else if clauses (well, mostly).

In order to solve the problem we are going to divide the problem space into two separate class hierarchies. We have identified an abstraction "Pay Model" and declared yet another interface to describe the behavior of the abstraction. PayModel is the highest level of abstraction in the second of the two class hierarchies, the other being Employee.

```
public interface PayModel
{
    public float calcEmployeeCost(Employee emp);
}
```

Notice that the method calcEmployeeCost() takes an Employee as a parameter. This means that the concrete classes implementing both Employee and PayModel can vary independently of the code written in terms of their interfaces.

Here are two concrete classes implementing `PayModel`, both containing a brief description of their respective behaviors:

```java
public final class SimplePayModel
  implements PayModel
{
  public float calcEmployeeCost(Employee emp)
  {
    //this model doesn't use any bonus calculations
    //but increases salaries by 15%
    return emp.getSalary()*1.15F;
  }
}

public final class IncentivePayModel
  implements PayModel
{
  public float calcEmployeeCost(Employee emp)
  {
    //this model uses number of sick days to
    //alter the annual bonus. Employees with
    //fewer than 5 sick days get an additional 10%

    float sal=emp.getSalary();
    float bonus=emp.calcAnnualBonus();
    int sick_days=emp.getDaysOffSick();

    float total_cost=sal;
    if(sick_days<5)
      total_cost+=(bonus*1.1);
    else if(sick_days>10) //lose 10% for being sick
      total_cost+=(bonus*.9);

    return total_cost;
  }
}
```

To see how this all hangs together, here is the modified `EmployeeOperations` utility class:

```java
public final class EmployeeOperations
{
  public static float calcCostOfEmployees(
    Enumeration employees,PayModel pay_model)
  {
    float total_cost=0F;
```

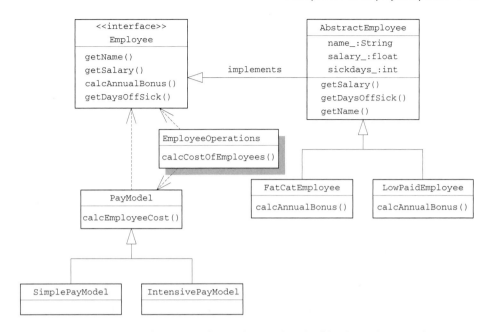

Figure 3.2 `Employee` and `PayModel` hierarchy used in double-dispatch example

```
    while(employees.hasMoreElements())
    {
        Employee emp=(Employee)employees.nextElement();
        //use the PayModel object to do the work
        total_cost+=pay_model.calcEmployeeCost(emp);
    }
    return total_cost;
    }
}
```

This design is very flexible, allowing any concrete `PayModel` to operate on any concrete `Employee`. As new `PayModels` are invented and new `Employee` types are added, the sample code in `calcCostOfEmployees()` remains unaltered.

Figure 3.2 shows the UML diagram for the two inheritance hierarchies that we have created.

The example below shows this in action using our two arbitrary concrete `PayModels` and `Employees`.

```
public static void main(String argv[])
{
    java.util.Vector emps= new java.util.Vector();
    emps.addElement( new FatCatEmployee("The Boss",500000,10));
    emps.addElement( new LowPaidEmployee("The Tea Boy",5000,1));

    PayModel pm1= new SimplePayModel();
    PayModel pm2= new IncentivePayModel();
```

```
float cost1=EmployeeOperations.calcCostOfEmployees(
  emps.elements(),pm1);
float cost2=EmployeeOperations.calcCostOfEmployees(
  emps.elements(),pm2);

System.out.println("SimplePayModel costs="+cost1);
System.out.println("InscentivePayModel costs="+cost2);
}
```

The technique illustrated above is known as a *double dispatch*, a technique that may crop up from time to time in the remaining chapters.

SUMMARY

In order to describe and understand polymorphism we need to differentiate between the apparent type of an object that we are using in client code, and the actual or real type of the underlying object. The behavior of the system will depend on the real type of the object.

This means that we can move type-specific behavior into the class responsible for implementing that type within an inheritance hierarchy. This is often referred to as specialization. If it is done in accord with a well-designed inheritance hierarchy, specialization results in better placement of methods and a large reduction in client constructs such as case statements and other forms of "type dependent" client code.

If we use polymorphism appropriately it has a profound effect on the structure of our design and greatly reduces the amount of code that needs to be written – this is sometimes referred as "code implosion."

When a polymorphic system becomes subject to the reintroduction of a switch or a series of condition statements to model complex type-based behavior, we can use the double-dispatch technique to model more than one type hierarchy, at the same time resolving the apparent problems.

A combination of interfaces and polymorphism is the source of a number of powerful and elegant idioms, as we shall see in some of the following chapters.

SECTION SUMMARY

Java's support for the OO fundamentals of abstraction, encapsulation, inheritance, and polymorphism make it an extremely popular and productive object-oriented programming environment. A clear understanding of these fundamentals is key to designing and implementing scalable and robust Java systems.

Encapsulation allows us to build systems that are more flexible, maintainable, and tolerant to change. Although the ideas of encapsulation are not unique to object-oriented systems, language features such as classes and interfaces allow designers and programmers to carry encapsulation concepts directly into the system source code. Code designed and implemented using these concepts should be less inter-dependent, or exhibit less "coupling." The many benefits to using encapsulation, include system stability and increased prospects for class reuse. An unexpected benefit is that as Java systems grow in complexity, runtime performance scales extremely well.

Interfaces are a very pure design and implementation tool. We encourage their use throughout the design and implementation process. Interfaces can be seen as the guarantees made between the various components of a Java system, be it single platform or distributed. It is strange but true that the reason interfaces are so powerful is what they leave out, not what they include. This Taoist-like notion is extremely hard to pin down in any formal way but the continual use of interfaces results in a deep understanding of their power and flexibility.

Inheritance allows us to build abstract hierarchies. Designing these hierarchies well is key to good object-oriented design. Strong abstraction skills do not come cheap and are normally hard won over many years, but our own experience and that of others stated in the form of patterns and language idioms means that over time we can produce elegant and realistic designs to solve practical problems in Java software.

Given that we have a well-designed inheritance hierarchy we can specialize class- or type-based behavior into the appropriate methods of the classes within our design. Polymorphism allows us to use this special behavior without having to know at any time the concrete type of a class. This means that Java can directly support abstraction-based programming, without the programmer having to worry about the underlying mechanics, although these need to be understood in order to build predictable and reliable Java systems.

The combination of the use of abstraction, encapsulation, inheritance, and polymorphism can result in huge reductions in the amount of code that we need to produce to solve a given problem. This is sometimes called the OO "code implosion." However, to really get the greatest benefit from these language features we must balance this advantage by spending more time in the design phase, to make sure that the overall structure of the system is coherent and adheres to a set of architectural principles set out in the system's design.

By now you should be fully equipped for what is to come. From here on in we assume you have grasped the concepts outlined in the first three introductory chapters, so from time to time it may be worth going back and reviewing them again. Now that you have become familiar with these basic principles we can start to combine them in various ways, which leads us on to examining the idioms that occur in well-designed object-oriented Java systems . . . .

4 Type safety and constants

Introduction

In this chapter we will be investigating constants and how we use "constant objects" in Java and introducing some Java idioms that can help reduce the risk of runtime errors. So hold onto your hat and prepare for a roller coaster ride ranging from constant primitive types via typesafe constants and how to make friends with your compiler, to an in-depth look at how to use immutable objects in Java.

Understanding constants

The idea of constants allows for greater expression in Java code by attaching a name to a particular state. For example, with an `int` that is used to represent the maximum number of fish in the fish tank we could use the following form:

```
final int MAXIMUM_NUMBER_OF_FISH = 10;
```

The use of the `final` keyword in this statement is to tell the compiler that it is the first and final value that a particular object reference will take – it can be initialized, but not assigned. Remember, that in the case of "blank" finals, the initialization does not have to happen at the same time as the declaration, but once the initialization has been made that's it. It is not possible to reassign a value to a `final` field or `final` local instance.

There are two major benefits that we gain from using constants straight out of the starting gate. The first is that our code becomes much more readable by others, avoiding the use of "magic" numbers that just appear in the code and do not mean anything to the reader, or leave the reader to work out what the number is being used for.

The second is that we can attach a value to many uses of the same constant. This allows us to keep our code more maintainable because there is only a single point of initialization for the value of the constant, although it may be used in many places within our code.

In some cases a `final` member will also be declared as a `static`. This makes it a `class` constant. If it is constant and we are only using it in the class methods, then it is not going to change with varying instances of the class, so it makes sense to have only one copy of the constant no matter how many class instances there are.

Probably our last consideration in terms of modifiers is whether the constant is for internal use by the class or for use by clients of our class. In the case below, the `final` class member is for external use:

```java
public class FishTank
{
    public static final int MAXIMUM_NUMBER_OF_FISH = 10;
    //
}
```

As the above constant value is declared `static` and `public` it can be accessed via the class.

To refer to the `MAXIMUM_NUMBER_OF_FISH` in the `FishTank` from other classes use the syntax

```java
FishTank.MAXIMUM_NUMBER_OF_FISH;
```

This form of constant in Java derives from C and C++. In C either the `enum` construct or `static` integers are commonly used to express constant values. Although Java is loosely based on C++ the designers of the Java language wisely chose not to include the `enum` construct. However, the C/C++ connection still exists in the form of the `static int`.

Here is an example from `java.awt.Font`:

```java
public class Font
{
    public final static int PLAIN = 0;
    public final static int BOLD = 1;
    public final static int ITALIC = 2;

    public Font(String name, int style, int size);
    //
}
```

Using primitive types such as integer to represent constants improves the readability of a program; however, consider the declaration of the two font objects being created below:

```java
Font font1=new Font("Helvetica",Font.BOLD,15);
Font font2=new Font("Helvetica",15,Font.BOLD);
```

Both of these declarations will compile successfully; however, font2 will cause a runtime error. Why is this? If you examine the declaration of the Font constructor you will see that it takes three parameters, a string and two integers. The first of the integer parameters is for the style of the font and the second for the point size. There is no way for the compiler to differentiate between the two parameters – any valid integer value may be passed in.

For example, your compiler will happily accept this kind of stupidity:

```
Font font3=
new Font("Helvetica", FishTank.MAXIMUM_NUMBER_OF_FISH,15);
```

This leaves the implementor of a class such as Font with the responsibility of range checking the Font style parameter. So we might try this:

```
if(style!= BOLD && style!= PLAIN && style!= ITALIC)
    //throw an exception
```

So now we are left with a problem. The need to range check or validate constants is essential when using this form. You may be thinking, "Well, that's not so terrible, we have always had to do some form of range checking." That may be so, but each time a new constant is added to your class you will need to update your validation method. A common way to help reduce the risk in classes whose constants have consecutive values, that can also be used to index an array, is to start from zero and have a constant representing the maximum value + 1, in the form:

```
public class ClassWithConstants
{
  public static final int MIN_CONSTS=0;
  public static final int CONST1=0;
  public static final int CONST2=1;
  public static final int MAX_CONSTS=2;

  //private helper method
  private void validateConstant( int constant )
    throws IllegalConstantException //defined elsewhere
  {
    if(constant<MIN_CONSTS || constant>=MAX_CONSTS)
      throw new IllegalConstantException();
  }
}
```

By introducing constant values that represent the upper and lower bounds of the range we have reduced the risk that range-checking methods become out of sync when new constants are added to the class. That is, as long as we remember to update MAX_CONSTS. Although this is an improvement it still leaves us with the risk of an IllegalArgumentException being thrown at runtime. Wouldn't it be cool if we could get the compiler to do the checking for us? Well, we can!

Those readers who see their compiler as a nagging in-law, always quick to pull you up on the slightest error, rejoicing in the ability to show you up in front of your friends or colleagues, will be surprised to learn that in fact your compiler is a good friend! Get to understand it and it is there to help you.

(T) Get your compiler to check that constants passed as parameters are valid.

There are two types of errors that can be present with the form of constants illustrated above:

- The need to perform range checking within methods is essential for a program to behave correctly.
- There is always that guy who gets lazy and remembers that, say, Font.BOLD is equal to 1 and writes code like this: Font font1= new Font("Helvetica",1,12) – a disaster if you ever reorder your constants!

To take advantage of the compiler's type-checking capabilities we need to create a constant that is an instance of a class rather than a primitive type such as int.

The listing below show our first attempt at doing this. We call this idiom "Typesafe constant."

Typesafe constant

```
public final class AlienRace
{
  public static final AlienRace BORG= new AlienRace();
  public static final AlienRace FERENGI= new AlienRace();

  private AlienRace() {}
}

public class Tester
{
  public static void test()
  {
    constTest(FishTank.MAXIMUM_NUMBER_OF_FISH); //error !!!
    constTest(AlienRace.FERENGI); //okay
  }

  public static void constTest( AlienRace alien )
  {
    //no range checking required
    if(alien==AlienRace.BORG)
      System.out.println("Resistance is futile");

    if(alien==AlienRace.FERENGI)
      System.out.println("A wife is a luxury," +
        "but a good accountant a necessity");
  }
}
```

Although it is highly unlikely that you will agree with either Borg or Ferengi culture, the example code illustrates how the compiler only allows instances of class `AlienRace` to be passed as parameters.

Let us take a closer look at class `AlienRace`:

- The class is declared `final` – this is to stop subclassing. If we allowed subclassing of class `AlienRace` we would end up back where we started, having to perform range checking because subclass instances could be passed to methods taking an `AlienRace` parameter.
- The constructor is `private` – this stops others from creating valid instances of the "constant" class.
- The class is self-referential – it contains instances of `AlienRace` objects.

As you can see from the `Tester` class, the resulting client code has the benefit of readability, but the implementor of the method:

```
public static void constTest( AlienRace alien )
```

does not have to perform any range checking because the compiler will only allow instances of `AlienRace` to be passed as parameters. We have made the constructor `private`, which means that we know that the only valid instances of class `AlienRace` are those that we have defined as `public static final` within the class.

We had successfully used this idiom for quite some time; however, we initially overlooked one case where the compiler's type checking could be circumnavigated and the model broken.

Consider this:

```
Tester.constTest( null );
```

which is almost as bad as `FishTank.MAXIMUM_NUMBER_OF_FISH` being passed to a `Font`!

There are two ways of approaching the problem:

- If another developer is daft enough to pass a null instead of a typesafe constant, simply let the Java runtime throw a `NullPointerException`. The rationale behind this approach is that it *is* an exceptional condition and should be treated that way.
- Use a proxy class to encapsulate a null constant. This second approach is illustrated below, but there is one caveat to adopting it. If the aforementioned "daft" developer passed a `null` value, what was his or her intention? What we are getting at here is that by wrapping a `null` in a proxy object, `null` can end up having more than one meaning.

Here is how to implement a null proxy in Java:

```
public final class AlienRace
{
  public static final AlienRace BORG= null;
  public static final AlienRace FERENGI= new AlienRace();

  private AlienRace() { }
}
```

The only difference here is that one of the public static final instance variables is initialized to null rather than a new instance. Overall this solves the problem for simple constants that have no state, but introduces another problem – how can we apply this to typesafe constants that have state, when one instance has to be null?

The listing below illustrates the problem – the null instance cannot have a value so any attempt to invoke AlienRace.BORG.GetValue() would result in the Java runtime "assimilating" your program by throwing a NullPointerException!

```
public final class AlienRace
{
    public static final AlienRace BORG= null; //can't call ctor
    public static final AlienRace FERENGI= new AlienRace(1);

    private int value_; //some state for the class

    private AlienRace(int value) //the ctor
    { value_ = value; }

    public int getValue()
    { return value_; }
}
```

To solve this problem we can use a proxy object to represent the constant. The UML diagram in Figure 4.1 shows the relationship between ConstProxy and AlienRace.

We use the proxy object to encapsulate the concept of a null constant.

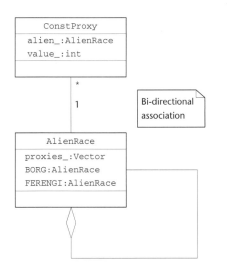

Figure 4.1 Typesafe constant using null proxy

```
class ConstProxy
{
    private AlienRace alien_;
    private int value_;
```

```java
  public ConstProxy(AlienRace alien, int value)
  {
    alien_=alien;
    value_=value;
  }

  public boolean isHolding(AlienRace alien)
  { return alien_ == alien; }

  public int getValue()
  { return value_; }
}

public final class AlienRace
{
  public static final AlienRace BORG= null;
  public static final AlienRace FERENGI= new AlienRace();

  private static Vector proxies_ = new Vector();

  static
  {
    proxies_.addElement( new ConstProxy(BORG,0) );
    proxies_.addElement( new ConstProxy(FERENGI,1) );
  }

  private AlienRace(){} //private ctor

  static int valueOf(AlienRace alien)
  {
    ConstProxy target = null;
    Enumeration e = proxies_.elements();
    while( e.hasMoreElements())
    {
        target = (ConstProxy)e.nextElement();
        if(target.isHolding( alien ) ) break;
    }
    return target.getValue();
  }
}
```

Here is an example of some client code using the updated `AlienRace` class:

```java
System.out.println("AlienRace.FERENGI has a value of " +
    AlienRace.ValueOf(AlienRace.FERENGI) )
```

which produces the following output:

```
AlienRace.FERENGI has a value of 1
```

By using the proxy technique it becomes possible to serialize typesafe constants by using their proxy class – remember that static instance variables are not serialized as they are class instance variables, not object instance variables.

"OK," you are thinking, "all this is great, but what is it going to cost me in terms of performance?" The 80–20 rule states that 80 percent of a program's execution time is spent in 20 percent of the code, so think carefully before making performance your top priority – a fast program is no use if it is prone to runtime errors. This section is really about using the compiler to make your programs safe, while remaining tolerant to change. In most of our work this is more important than out-and-out performance. However, for those of you worried, here is some information that might help in that decision.

For a static final int the compiler generates code that is equivalent to an inline comparison because the value of the static final int is known at compile time. So for example:

```
if(var==FishTank.MAX)   /*becomes*/   if (var==10)
```

whereas for a typesafe constant the compiler will generate code that loads the static object reference and then perform a comparison between that object reference and the object in the condition statement.

Before we leave the topic of constants it is worth considering why class java.awt.Font used static final int(s) as constants. This was to allow for styles to be combined in the form (Font.BOLD | Font.ITALIC). In many cases the same effect can be achieved by using explicit typesafe constants such as MyFont.BOLD_ITALIC.

Immutable objects

Having examined constants in some depth let us now extend constants to the full-blown object model by describing immutable objects. These objects are ones that cannot be changed after construction. An example of an immutable object is java.lang.String. Once a String has been initialized there is no way to alter the internal representation of the object. So if we declare String str= "I'll never change"; and then pass it to the method below, we can be assured that str will be unaltered after the method has returned, because class String does not have any methods that you can use to modify its value.

```
public void tryToAlterString( String s )
{
  s="I've changed"; //or have I ?
}
```

The method tryToAlterString() may give the impression that the value of s has been altered; however, when an object is passed to a method, it is actually a copy of a reference to that object, not the actual object. So in the above example the value "I've changed" is being assigned to a local object reference, not the original object. You can guard against this type of misleading code by declaring the parameter as final.

Declare method parameters as final when you want to guard against meaningless object reference assignment.

```
public void tryToAlterString( final String s )
{
  s="I've changed";  //compiler error
}
```

The use of final in this context ensures that you do not accidentally attempt to modify an object reference, which as you have just seen has no effect to the calling code, but might have a side effect on the logic within the method if it goes unchecked. While we are on the subject of final method parameters, if we were to instantiate an anonymous inner class that used a non-final method parameter we would get a compiler error.

```
public void method(String str)
{
  Runnable r= new Runnable()
  {
    public void run()
    {
      System.out.println(str); //compiler error!
    }
  };

  Thread t= new Thread(r);
  t.start();
}
```

This is easily resolved by declaring the method as

```
public void method(final String str) {...}
```

or declaring a local variable as final:

```
public void method(String str)
{
  final String copyRef=str;
  Runnable r= new Runnable()
  {
    public void run()
    {
      System.out.println(copyRef); //OK
    }
  };
  //as before
}
```

There are other contexts in which we need mutable objects to act as immutable.

Consider the methods below in the class DatePrinter. Both take an object reference to a Calendar. Imagine that someone else has written the DatePrinter class and you happily invoke the method printNextDaysDate(final Calendar calendar) with an instance of Calendar that you are using to store today's date.

```
public class DatePrinter
{
  public void printDate( Calendar calendar )
  {
    String dateStr="";
    //get the date and format the string
    System.out.println(dateStr);
  }

  public void printNextDaysDate( final Calendar calendar )
  {
    String dateStr="";
    //the next line modifies the orginal object
    calendar.roll(Calendar.DAY_OF_MONTH,true); //oops
    //get the date from the calendar and format the string
    System.out.println(dateStr);
  }
}
```

Although it may not be immediately apparent, the author of printNextDaysDate() has side effected the calendar parameter, by calling roll(), which could easily lead to subtle bugs in the calling code. This side effecting occurs because all Java method object parameters are passed by reference and not by value, allowing any accessible methods to be invoked. Also note that the use of the final method parameter does not help us here.

These kinds of subtle errors can be tricky to track down in large systems so we need to come up with a strategy to help us avoid this problem. Notice that the use of final in the method parameter declarations does not stop you invoking methods that alter the state of calendar, it only stops reassignment of a copy of the object reference.

You can protect against accidental side effects either by implementing a read-only interface or by using cloning.

Implementing a read-only interface

In this idiom we are again using Java interfaces. In this case it is to provide a subset of the operations on the class Date which we developed in an earlier chapter. This will allow us access to only those operations that cannot change the state of any Date object.

 Use a read-only interface to make a mutable object act as immutable.

```
public interface ReadOnlyDate
{
  public int getTodaysDate();
}

public class Date implements ReadOnlyDate
{
  public int getTodaysDate()
  { /* return the date */ }

  public void incDay(int i)
  { /*move date on by a number of days */ }

  // ... other methods etc.
}
```

By introducing a "read-only" interface you can protect your objects against unintentional mutation which is nasty at the best of times. For example:

```
public void printNextDaysDate( ReadOnlyDate date )
{
  String dateStr="";
  date.incDay(1);  //compiler error,
  //not in ReadOnlyDate interface
  //format the string
  System.out.println(dateStr);
}
```

By changing the parameter to a ReadOnlyDate the implementor cannot accidentally side effect the object. This will be enforced by the compiler – didn't we tell you it was a good friend?

Returning object references to instance fields is as risky as passing mutable objects as parameters to methods. We are simply weakening class encapsulation in one of the two directions. So we also use the read-only interface technique for accessor methods that return read-only versions of objects, as follows:

```
// Return a date field reference that a client can't change
public ReadOnlyDate getDate ()
{ return date_; }
```

One question that may be occurring to you is that although this technique is very fine for classes that we are writing ourselves, what about adding immutability to a class that already exists in another package such as Panel from the AWT? In this case we can use the Adapter pattern, through inheritance:

```
interface ReadOnlyPanel
{
  public Dimension getSize();
  //other read only operations
}
```

```
public class PanelAdapter extends Panel
  implements ReadOnlyPanel
{ }
```

or we can use delegation:

```
public class PanelDelegator
  implements ReadOnlyPanel
{
  private Panel panel_;
  public PanelDelegator(Panel panel)
  {
    panel_=panel;
  }
  //use delegation in methods declared in ReadOnlyPanel
  public Dimension getSize() { return panel_.getSize(); }
}
```

Delegation has the advantage for classes that have numerous constructors and few methods, whereas inheritance is better for classes with few constructors and many read-only methods.

Another approach to avoiding these nasty mutations is to use cloning.

Cloning

Before we start investigating cloning, let us first examine why we need it in the first place. In Chapters 2 and 3 we discuss polymorphism and interfaces and their respective roles in Java and OO design. In a polymorphic system, objects contain and use references to other objects based on their abstract type, or interface.

The UML diagram in Figure 4.2 shows that the class Factory can make a reference to an object that implements the interface Product. Classes Product1 and Product2 both implement Product.

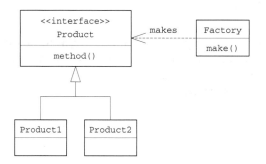

Figure 4.2 Factory example

```
public class Factory
{
  public Product make(/* make params */)
  {
    return new Product1();
  }
}

public class CopyTest
{
  public static void main(String args[])
  {
    Factory factory = new Factory();
    Product prod1=factory.make();
    Product prod2=prod1; //reference assignment
  }
}
```

In the class `CopyTest()` the `main` method has a local variable `prod1` which could be a reference to any instance of a class that implements `Product`. The line `prod2=prod1` assigns a copy of a reference, but what if we wanted to take a copy of the actual object? How could this be done when `main()` has no knowledge of the concrete type? A *bad* way to attempt to do this would be to use `instanceof` to determine the runtime type of the object and then to cast to the appropriate type before copying via its accessor methods. There are many reasons why this is bad; here are just a few:

• The client code would have to know about all the concrete types.

• Accessor methods generally only export some of the object's properties.

• This is not object-oriented.

To solve the problem OO designers came up with a pattern now known as "Prototype" – this pattern is implemented in Java as an idiom through the method `java.lang.Object.clone()`.

"Hang on," you are thinking "what's all the fuss about if `java.lang.Object` has a `clone()` method – surely we could just use that?" Well, you would be partly correct, but the default implementation for `Object.clone()` is to throw a `CloneNotSupported Exception`.

Java does however provide a mechanism for telling the compiler to perform a shallow, or field-for-field, copy when `clone()` is called. You indicate this by declaring your class as implementing `java.lang.Cloneable`.

```
public interface java.lang.Cloneable { }
```

This interface is empty, but tells the compiler to generate the code for a shallow copy if the method is called. Most of the compilers we have tested expect you to provide a `clone()` implementation that calls `super.clone()`, whereas others simply generate the code for you.

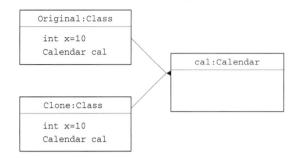

Figure 4.3 Shallow copy

(**T**) Understand the difference between shallow and deep copying.

Before you rush off and paste the text implements java.lang.Cloneable into all your class declarations it is important to understand a couple more things.

1. How each instance variable (field) should be copied. By using a deep copy or a shallow copy?

   A shallow copy is a field-for-field copy. If a field is an object reference the cloned object also has a reference to the same object (Figure 4.3). Updates to the referenced object(s) are reflected in the copied object.

   A deep copy occurs when clone() is also called on any object references within the object being cloned (Figure 4.4). Sorry, but this time you are on your own – you have to implement this for yourself.

2. What your compiler expects from you.

   We have noted inconsistencies across all the compilers we have tested, therefore the code samples here are ones which work on all the compilers we have tested.

As most of the compilers we have tested expect you to provide a clone() implementation that calls super.clone() and this code is the same for every class that

Figure 4.4 Deep copy

you want to support the default (shallow) cloning, you may want to consider reusing a superclass that supports this default behavior. For example:

```
public class CloneableObject implements Cloneable
{
  public Object clone()
  {
    Object clone=null;
    try
    {
      clone = super.clone();
    }
    catch (CloneNotSupportedException ex)
    {
      //this should not occur
      throw new InternalError( ex.toString() );
    }
    return clone;
  }
}
```

If `CloneableObject` did not implement `Cloneable` the call to `super.clone()` would result in a `CloneNotSupportedException`.

Earlier we posed the question, "How could an instance of `Product` be cloned?" The answer – you simply declare the concrete `Product` as extending our `CloneableObject` and add `public Object clone()` to the `Product` interface.

```
public interface Product
{
  public void method();
  public Object clone();
}

public interface Product1 extends CloneableObject
  implements Product
{
  //private instance variables etc.
  public void method();
}
```

This is sufficient for the compiler to provide the default shallow copy; however, if the concrete class `Product1` contains references to other objects you must consider whether a deep copy is required or not. To implement a deep copy simply provide an implementation for `clone()` in the concrete class, explicitly calling `clone()` on each object instance variable.

```
public class Product1
  implements Product, Cloneable
```

```
{
  //instance variables
  private Calendar calendar_;

  private Product1() {} //empty private ctor
  public Product1(/* params */) { }

  public Object clone()
  {
    Product1 p1=new Product1();  //using private ctor
    p1.calendar_=calendar_.clone();  //deep copy
    return p1;
  }
}
```

A point to note here is that if `Calendar` did not support `clone()` your only option may be to use a shallow copy or attempt to copy the object via its accessor methods.

Here are two places that you will need to support `clone()` in your classes:

- In classes whose instances are likely to be passed as parameters.

- If another object needs to cache the current state of an instance of the class (see Memento pattern).

Be careful to document the policy you decide upon because if you do not, you could either end up with the implementor of the method taking a `clone()` upon entry and the client taking a `clone()` before calling the method, or neither. If too much cloning takes place, a significant and unnecessary overhead will be introduced. A little later in this chapter, we offer a way of addressing this issue.

Just to round off our tour of the clones you might want to know that you can also use the `clone()` method on an array but, as ever, it is a shallow copy by default.

Cloneable ReadOnly Object

Documenting and deciding upon a policy to use for cloning can be difficult, as we have already discussed, and will be even harder to achieve on a practical, non-trivial project. By using cloning and defining a read-only interface we can achieve immutable object parameters that can be cloned if required.

The listing below illustrates this technique for `java.util.Calendar`. Although this example uses a Java library class the technique works equally well for any class. We are using the delegation approach here as `java.util.Calendar` has many constructors and our `ReadOnlyCalendar` has only one method.

```
public interface ReadOnlyCalendar
{
  public int get(int type);
  public Object clone();
}
```

```
public final class ReadOnlyCalendarImpl
  implements ReadOnlyCalendar, Cloneable
{
  private Calendar calendar_;
  public ReadOnlyCalendarImpl(Calendar cal)
  {
    calendar_=cal;
  }
  public int get(int type)
  {
    return calendar_.get(type);
  }
  public Object clone()
  {
    return calendar_.clone();
  }
}
```

By using this technique you can safely pass objects that appear immutable to methods as parameters, without the fear of side effecting (caveat: as long as clone() is implemented properly). For example, if the implementor of the method PrintNext DaysDate() in class DatePrinter really needs to use Calendar.roll() he or she can, by invoking ReadOnlyCalendar.clone() first.

```
//updated with read only and cloneable parameter
public void PrintNextDaysDate( ReadOnlyCalendar date )
{
  String dateStr="";
  Calendar calCopy=(Calendar)date.clone();
  calCopy.roll(Calendar.DATE,true);
  //no side effects
  //format the string
  System.out.println(dateStr);
}
```

The Cloneable ReadOnly Object idiom offers the following advantages:

- Removes the risk of "over-cloning."
- Allows for mutable objects to be passed as immutable parameters.
- Places responsibility on the method implementor to do the cloning.

We have intentionally used delegation in this last example to illustrate the trade-off between using inheritance, which requires constructors to explicitly call their super-class, and delegation which requires the Adapter class to delegate to its implementation class. Purists could argue that clone() is misleading in our class ReadOnlyCalendarImpl as it returns a clone of Calendar and not of itself. Using inheritance instead of delegation would satisfy this argument.

SUMMARY

The underlying motive for using constants is to reduce unwanted changes to the state of objects. This results in more stable and reliable systems.

It is possible to define interfaces that reduce the number of methods available to clients of a class in such a way that it is much less likely that an object's state can be perturbed in an unexpected or malicious way. If an interface only allows a class to be "read" rather than updated this can be called a read-only interface.

Using interfaces allows us to catch these errors at compile time which is a positive use of the Java compiler's "pedantic" error-checking policy. By extending these basic concepts we have been able to implement *Typesafe constants* and *Cloneable ReadOnly Objects*.

5 Exceptions

Introduction

In the last chapter we examined how to use constants and other constant-based idioms to spot errors at compile time in order to build more reliable and maintainable systems. Spotting potential errors at compile time is always preferable to runtime checks; however, some types of problems can only be identified at runtime, such as network errors and memory exhaustion.

In this chapter we will be looking at error handling strategies which will help to make your programs handle these runtime problems. Fortunately the Java language has built-in mechanisms for handling runtime issues, namely throwables of which there are two major types: errors and exceptions. Because exceptions are used extensively in Java, we refer to this system as an exception mechanism although throwables can also be used to handle errors, of course.

Programming languages that do not support a true exception mechanism are more prone to unpredictable runtime errors because clients of library functions or methods are at liberty to ignore error codes returned or flags set by these functions or methods. The same is equally true of Java programs that do not use the language's exception mechanism.

Classical error handling

Classically programmers have used error flags or return values from methods to indicate a failure such as invalid parameters or out of memory errors. Regardless of how conscientious an implementor of a method may be in making sure that if an error occurs, a sensible value is returned, there is no way of ensuring that the client checks that value. Consider the following class which has two methods. One method opens a database with a given name and returns a boolean value to indicate success/failure. The second method, getEmployees(), checks if the database has been opened successfully and then performs the work to get the employees.

```
public class Database
{
  public boolean open(String name)
  {
    boolean ok_=false;
    //attempt to open database
    //if open ok_==true
    return ok_;
  }
  public void close() {...}
  public Enumeration getEmployees(String filter)
  {
    Enumeration e=null;
    //if database is open get employees

    return e;
  }
}
```

By using the classical approach to error handling a client of class Database is at liberty to write code like this:

```
Database db= new Database();
String filter="age>20";
db.open("emp_db");
Enumeration e=db.getEmployees(filter);
if(e==null)
System.out.println("No employees found matching
   filter "+filter);
```

If you examine the client code you will notice that the return value from open() is not checked, resulting in getEmployee() returning null. To the client of class Database in this example the null return probably indicates that no employees were found matching the given filter. This is obviously incorrect and misleading both to the client of class Database and ultimately the end user of this program. To work predictably the client code should have been written as follows:

```
if(db.open("emp_db"));
{
  //execute code above
}
else
{
  //report error
}
```

Unfortunately with the classical approach to error handling there is no way to enforce that error flags are checked.

There are several possible reasons why the author of the client code did not check the return code from the `open()` method. Perhaps it was laziness, they did not know they had to, or it was intentional in order to optimize the code by removing the error checking.

Although this example may produce misleading results to the user, it is not fatal. However, if the client code forgets to check error codes when a database transaction is involved, the integrity of the database is likely to suffer, leaving it in an inconsistent state. Consider the method sequence below where only part of the transaction succeeded, but the client code did not check returned error codes!

```
start transaction    //okay
update 1             //okay
update dependencies  //failed, but error code not checked
commit               //oops
```

As you can see, the classical approach to error handling is flawed in that it is susceptible to two types of problems. In the first case you cannot ensure that a client of a class checks the return code for error conditions raised in its methods.

Or in the second case, simply the reverse, in which the error condition is double-checked. The implementor of a method checks that everything is OK and so does the client, which is better from a correctness point of view but results in extremely inefficient code.

In languages that require the programmer to handle memory allocation and deletion, the lack of a robust error handling strategy often results in program failures due to access violations or core dumps. Thankfully Java inherently checks for memory violations and is extremely safe from this perspective; however, we can use exceptions to guard against a host of other runtime problems.

Java's exceptions

The Java language has built-in features to help you write more robust systems, so if you have come to Java from another language now is the time to stop writing code that uses the classical approach and get your head around the concept of throwing and catching exceptions.

There are two kinds of exceptions in Java which are either user-defined exceptions (explicit) or those that are implicitly defined by the Java environment – runtime exceptions. Implicit or runtime exceptions occur when your code performs an illegal operation such as division by zero in integer calculations or attempting to invoke a method using a `null` object reference.

Your favorite Java reference manual will have all the information you need about runtime exceptions, so for the rest of this chapter we will concentrate on explicit exceptions, the ones that "we" the programmers define and throw.

So how do exceptions differ from the classical approach? When an exception is thrown the Java Virtual Machine (JVM) will look for an exception handler within the current method; if one is found matching the exception type, control of the method is transferred to this handler. If, on the other hand, a handler is not found the JVM will unwind the call stack, checking each method on the stack for an appropriate handler until one is found or the program exits. Do not worry if that all sounds a bit too close to the spark-plugs for you; by the end of this chapter you will be wondering why you had not embraced exceptions earlier. So let us waste no more time and start to get our hands dirty.

Defining exceptions

As you can see from the UML diagram in Figure 5.1, all exceptions must be subclasses of `java.lang.Throwable`. In our database example we have started to add exceptions to alleviate some of the problems that we have described. The first stage was to declare an explicit exception `DbOpenFailureException` which is a subclass of `java.lang.Exception`, which itself extends `Throwable`.

The intention of this development is that when a client invokes the `open()` method on an instance of the `Database` class, and it fails, a `DbOpenFailureException` will be thrown. The `String` parameter to the constructor is used to pass a meaningful message back to the caller of `open()`. This can be seen as the "reason" for the exception.

```
public class DbOpenFailureException extends Exception
{
  public DbOpenFailureException(String reason)
  {
    super(reason);
  }
}
```

Having defined our `DbOpenFailureException` we now need to update the `open()` method to throw this exception on failure. The Java language has a very powerful model for exceptions, forcing all methods that throw explicit exceptions to declare them in the method declaration in the form

return_type method_name(parameters)
   ***throws** list_of_exception_types*

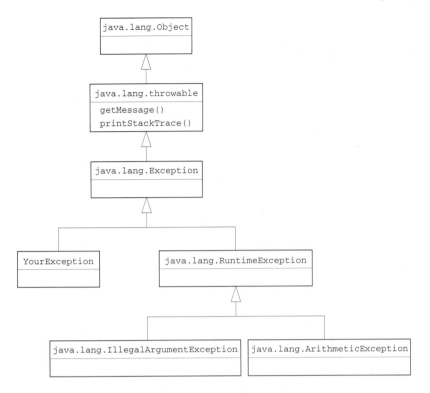

Figure 5.1 Java's exception hierarchy

Some other languages that support exceptions do not ensure that exceptions are caught at either compile time or runtime which can result in the same kind of problems as are associated with the classical approach. Here is the open() method redefined to make use of the Java exception mechanism:

```
public void open()
   throws DbOpenFailureException
{
   if(unableToOpen) //can't open the db so throw our exception
     throw new DbOpenFailureException("reason");
}
```

Using this definition, if we were to go back and try to recompile the client code that uses the Database object the compiler would tell us that "DbOpenFailureException not caught or declared by *calling method name*." Why is this?

If you recall, the problem with the classical approach is that there is no way to enforce that clients check returned error codes. All the Java compiler is doing here is helping us to write robust code. In effect it is saying that the method you are calling may throw an exception so "what are you going to do about it?"! You have two choices: either you handle the exception in the calling method or you declare that your method throws the same type of exception, passing the responsibility for handling the exception up the call stack. This is the really cool thing about Java's exceptions – you cannot just ignore them. For now we will concentrate on handling the exception in the calling method, but later in the chapter we will be looking at various other strategies.

Handling exceptions

Java has three keywords for handling exceptions: try, catch, and finally. A try block surrounds the code that may throw an exception and the catch block(s) are used to actually handle the exception types that may be thrown. Ignoring finally for the time being, the client code using the Database.open() method now looks like this:

```
try
{
   String filter= "age>20";
   db.open("emp_db");
   Enumeration e=db.getEmployees(filter);
   //process employees returned
}
catch(DbOpenFailureException ex)
{
   //handle the exception
   ex.printStackTrace();
}
```

Even with this very simple example you should immediately be able to see the benefits. The client code is forced to use exception handling and if an exception is thrown in the open() method, flow control transfers to the catch block of code where it can be dealt with.

Before we go any further it is worth pointing out that we could have written the catch clause in the above example as follows:

```
catch(Exception ex) {...}
```

or

```
catch(Throwable ex){...}
```

These are the most generic of all exception handlers, but we would strongly advise against using this form as it can easily be abused. We have seen many real-world code examples where developers just put a try/catch (Exception ex) around their code and hope for the best!

Catch as many exceptions as possible explicitly – avoid catch(Exception) as the only exception handler.

Now you have well and truly got the bug (wrong word!) for exceptions, your next thoughts should be turning to the getEmployees() method and how it should handle various error conditions.

We can put error conditions into two basic categories:

- Fatal errors – those from which the program cannot recover.

- Recoverable errors – resulting from conditions such an invalid user entry.

The category of the error condition will determine how the client code handles the resulting exception. If the database in our example is unavailable, perhaps because the server has been taken offline, the best course of action is to inform the user and proceed by gracefully closing down the client program – this is a fatal error condition. On the other hand, if a user enters a date and your Date class throws an exception because it is invalid, the probable course of action is to inform the user so they can re-enter the date, not exit the program – this is a recoverable error.

With this in mind let us categorize the possible error conditions for the getEmployees() method:

Fatal	Recoverable
Database not open	Filter parameter is invalid
	Persistent objects locked

Our table indicates that we require two new exception classes for the recoverable conditions. Assuming that we have implemented these, the updated version of getEmployees() would look like this:

```
public Enumeration getEmployees(String filter)
    throws DbOpenFailureException, InvalidFilterException,
      ObjectsLockedException
{
  Enumeration e=null;
  //if database has not been opened
  throw new DbOpenFailureException("Db not open!");

  //if invalid filter syntax
  throw new InvalidFilterException("Invalid filter: "+filter);

  //if attempt to get read lock fails
  throw new ObjectsLockedException("Read lock failed!");

  //get the employees and return iterator
  return e;
}
```

As you can see, this categorization allows us to be very clear about the types of exceptions to be thrown at each stage of the operations of the database. It is always a good idea to identify potential error conditions during the design phase and build your exception classes accordingly. This can clarify designs and simplify implementations.

P   Identify exception classes during the design phase.

Having looked at the source of the exceptions, now let us turn to the client code that uses the database. We could take several approaches to dealing with these exceptions; we have chosen to look at three of these possible approaches:

- Handle each exception on a per method call basis.
- Add exception handling for the new types in the same scope as before.
- Place exception handling for the new exceptions around getEmployees().

The first approach should almost always be avoided as it results in code like this:

```
try
{
  db.open("emp_db");
}
catch(DbOpenFailureException ex){/*handle ex*/}
try
{
  db.getEmployees("age>20");
}
catch(DbOpenFailureException ex){/*handle ex*/}
catch(InvalidFilterException ex){/*handle ex*/}
catch(ObjectsLockedException ex){/*handle ex*/}

db.close(); //is this open?, may throw exception too
```

Not only is the code incredibly difficult to read, let alone maintain, but it leads to many problems. For example, how can you call close() on the database if you cannot tell if it has been opened? OK, you could have a flag, but that would be introducing another level of complexity. As a general rule:

P   Avoid using try{...}catch{...} on a per method basis for all methods within a block.

Having dismissed the first approach, how about the second?

If we were to place the exception handling for getEmployees() in the outermost block, the thread of control would exit from the try block when a recoverable exception occurred, removing the option to recover from it!

```
try
{
  db.open("emp_db");
  db.getEmployees("age>20");
  //can't retry if lock not available and an exception occurs
}
catch(DbOpenFailureException ex){/*handle exp*/}
catch(InvalidFilterException ex){/*handle exp*/}
catch(ObjectsLockedException ex){/*handle exp*/}
```

Finally, it would make sense to use the third approach as it separates the fatal error condition (DbOpenFailureException) from the recoverable error conditions InvalidFilterException and ObjectLockedException as illustrated below:

```
try
{
  String filter="age>20";
  db.open("emp_db");
  try
  {
    Enumeration e=db.getEmployees(filter);
    //process employees returned
  }
  catch(InvalidFilterException ex)
  {
    //act
  }
  catch(ObjectsLockedException ex)
  {
    //act, maybe retry later?
  }
  //other method calls on db
  db.close();
}
catch(DbOpenFailureException ex)
{
  //handle the exception
  //let user know then exit ?
}
```

In this updated example the fatal error condition DbOpenFailureException is handled at the outermost scope whereas the recoverable exceptions are handled closer to their source, allowing appropriate actions to be taken according to the exception type.

(T) Separate fatal and non-fatal exception class hierarchies.

The code above seems to be quite a good solution, but it is already becoming very messy, and just consider how this simple example would evolve when we start adding other new exception classes for updating the database and other features.

Earlier we used a small table to show the potential error conditions that could occur in the getEmployees() method and noted which were fatal or recoverable conditions. If our Database class was a full production component it would have methods such as startTransaction(), endTransaction(), commit(), and rollback() plus various methods for retrieving objects.

If we were to make a list of all possible error conditions for our "production" version of Database, categorizing them into fatal and recoverable, we would end up

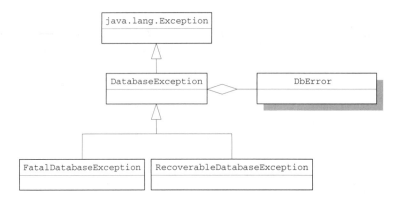

Figure 5.2 Exception hierarchy using a typesafe constant as state

with a whole heap of exception classes. As with all designs, the more classes, the more complicated and harder to maintain the resulting system will become. What we need is an encapsulated approach which does not compromise the robustness.

Reduce the overall number of exception classes by categorizing them and using a constant (typesafe) to represent the condition.

Putting our exception-based principles into action we end up with the exception class hierarchy for our Database class shown in Figure 5.2.

Some designs will require a further subclassing of domain-specific exception classes, but this is not required for our Database class. In our new design, the reason for the exception has become a typesafe constant of type DbFault in its own right rather than a simple string.

Here is how our DatabaseException looks where DbFault is a typesafe constant held as an instance field within the exception:

```
public class DatabaseException extends Exception
{
  private DbFault reason_;

  public DatabaseException(String why, DbFault err)
  {
    super(why);
    reason_=err;
  }
  public final DbFault getReasonCode() { return reason_;}
}
```

The classes FatalDatabaseException and RecoverableDatabaseException simply extend DatabaseException. Subclassing without specialization is usually to be avoided as it is better expressed as *"instance of"* rather than *"is a type of."* However, in this case we want to be able to use Java's exception handling capabilities to differentiate between fatal and recoverable conditions based on their type, without having to interrogate the `DatabaseException` via its `getReasonCode()` method. The exception `ObjectLockedException` introduced earlier would now be represented as follows:

```
throw new RecoverableDatabaseException
("Requested objects are locked",DbFault.READ_LOCK_FAILED);
```

Another approach, which does not use a `reason_` instance field, is to subclass `DatabaseException` further and catch at that level in the hierarchy to reduce the number of catch clauses. For example:

```
catch(DatabaseException ex)
{
  if(ex instanceof ObjectsLockedException)
  {
    //act
  }
  //else if ...
}
```

The problem with this approach is that we go back to producing far too many potential exception classes and end up with many uses of the `instanceof` keyword, resulting in complex and slow code. At this point we can discount this idea and go back to our middle ground solution.

Here is the client code that uses our new form of exception classes.

```
Enumeration testGetEmployees(Database db,
    String filter, int retries)
    throws FatalDatabaseException, RecoverableDatabaseException
{
  int count=0;
  while(count<retries)
  {
    try
    {
      //can throw FatalDatabaseException
      return db.getEmployees(filter);
    }
    catch(RecoverableDatabaseException ex)
    {
      DbFault reason= ex.getReasonCode();
      if(reason==DbFault.READ_LOCK_FAILED)
      {
        //wait, then
        count++;
      }
      else
        throw ex; //rethrow the non-fatal exception
    }
  }
```

```
    String msg="Failed after "+count+ "attempts";
    throw new RecoverableDatabaseException(msg,
        DbFault.READ_LOCK_FAILED);
}
```

The calling method of `testGetEmployees()` has the option to let a `FatalDatabase Exception` propagate up the call stack, but handle a `NonFatalDatabaseException`, such as `INVALID_FILTER`, and act accordingly. For example, if the calling method passed a filter provided by the user into `testGetEmployees()`, the calling method could be written to inform the user so they could try again.

In this code we have introduced an important feature of Java's exception handling that we have not mentioned before – the ability to throw an exception that has already been thrown. Catching and rethrowing exceptions is extremely useful for adding additional information about the exception on its way back up the call stack.

In the example above, `testGetEmployees()` is a wrapper around the Database method `getEmployees()`, but it allows for multiple retries if an object lock cannot be obtained; in this method only `READ_LOCK_FAILED` exceptions are handled, other `RecoverableDatabaseExceptions` are rethrown. There is one potential flaw in this example. If a client of this method invokes `printStackTrace()` on the exception, it will report that it originated from `getEmployees()`; although this is true we may want to indicate that the exception resulted from a failure in `testGetEmployees()`. The class `Throwable` provides a method `fillInStackTrace()` to facilitate the rethrowing of exceptions and altering the stack trace information. We could therefore rewrite that part of `getTestEmployees()` as follows:

```
throw (RecoverableException)ex.fillInStackTrace();
```

`fillInStackTrace()` is defined in class `Throwable` and returns an instance of `Throwable` with the stack trace information filled in with the current stack context. You need to cast the `Throwable` object to the actual exception type otherwise the compiler will insist that you have not declared or handled a `Throwable`.

We will be returning to our Database example later in this chapter when we introduce an new idiom called Delegated exception handling, but before we get there let us fill in some of the gaps.

Software designers from a structured background often find the use of exceptions unpalatable as there is not a single entry and single exit point from a method. It is almost possible to follow this golden rule of software engineering; however, the resulting code often ends up being more complex and harder to maintain, which defeats the original goal.

Single Entry Single Exit idiom

In order for this idiom to work it is necessary to declare that the method throws "Exception" (in fact that is all you need to declare, but that is a bad idea as you will see later on). This can lead to a cascade effect up the call stack.

```
void testGetEmployees( ... )
  throws FatalDatabaseException, RecoverableDatabaseException,
    Exception
{
  Exception ex=null;
  Enumeration emps=null; //assign employees to this
  //as before
  while(count<retries && ex==null && emps==null)
  {
    //as before, but assign caught exceptions
    //rather than throwing them and assign them
    //to the variable 'ex'
  }
  if(emps==null)
    ex = new RecoverableDatabaseException(...);

  if(ex!=null)
    throw ex;

  return emps;
}
```

Well, there you have it. The choice is yours!

Finally

While on the subject of returning elegantly from methods it is an appropriate time to introduce the third of the Java exception handling keywords, finally. The finally block of code is always executed even if an exception occurs in the preceding try block. In the example below, even though an exception is thrown in the try block, the finally block will always be executed, unless of course, you called System.exit() successfully in the preceding catch block.

```
void finallyTest()
{
  try
  {
    throw new Exception("Finally test");
  }
  catch(Exception ex)
  {
    ex.printStackTrace();
  }
  finally
  {
    System.out.println("***finally executed***");
  }
}
```

This code produces the following output when called from `main()` as a member of class `Test`:

```
java.lang.Exception: Finally test
        at Test.finallyTest
        at Test.main
***finally executed***
```

Just for the record, you can also have a `finally` clause without a `catch` clause.

(P) Never let exceptions propagate out of a `finally` block.

The method below, `lostExceptionTest()`, exhibits some very strange behavior. Examine the code carefully before moving on to the explanation that follows.

```
void lostExceptionTest()
  throws Exception
{
  try
  {
    //this exception gets lost
    throw new Exception("first exception");
  }
  finally
  {
    System.out.println("***finally executed***");
    //this exception propagates
    throw new Exception("second exception");
  }
}
```

This produces the output:

```
***finally executed***
java.lang.Exception: second exception
        at Test.lostExceptionTest
        at Test.main
```

(P) Never declare `throws Exception`. Always use a subclass of `Exception`.

In the method `lostExceptionText()` we have explicitly thrown an exception in the `finally` block; however, it is easy to become unstuck if you invoke a method in a `finally` block that throws an exception of the same type as one of those listed in the method's throws declaration, because the compiler will not issue an error! Therefore if your method's throws declaration includes `Exception` (or `Throwable`), the compiler will not tell you if a method you are invoking in `finally` throws an exception. There are two approaches to avoiding lost exceptions as highlighted above. Never declare that a method throws `Exception` and always catch exceptions in `finally`.

Using exceptions in constructors

Constructors allow the implicit initialization of objects. We generally use constructors and sometimes the static initializer to make sure an object is in a stable state when new is called. In a following chapter we look at the subject of creating and removing objects but for the moment it is relevant in this chapter to look at what happens if an exception propagates out of a constructor. By the way, you cannot let exceptions propagate out of a static initializer.

In the example below, class CtThrower throws an exception of type CtEx in its constructor. We have broken one of the rules established earlier and placed the exception handler around the call to new CtThrower to reiterate the importance of that rule and illustrate what happens when an exception propagates out of a constructor.

```
CtThrower ct=null;
try
{
  ct = new CtThrower();
}
catch(CtEx ex) { ex.printStackTrace();}

ct.someMethod(); //oops NullPointerException
```

As an exception is thrown in the constructor of class CtThrower the new operator does not return; instead control transfers to the matching exception handler.

Understand the implications of throwing exceptions in constructors.

The ability to throw exceptions from constructors is a powerful one as long as you are careful in your implementation of the constructor in question. Consider the FileCopier class below whose constructor takes two String arguments, for the source/destination file names:

```
public class FileCopier
{
  public FileCopier(String source,String dest)
    throws FileCopierEx
  {
    // attempt to open the source file
    // catch IOException and throw FileCopierEx
    // attempt to open the destination file
    // catch IOException and throw FileCopierEx
  }
}
```

A potential problem exists here. What happens if the source file opens OK and the destination file does not? Your first thought may be to use a finally block as you know it is guaranteed to be executed, but be careful: finally is always executed, so do not just place your tidy-up code there, otherwise the files will be opened and closed before the constructor returns!

While on the subject of object construction and destruction, finalize() can throw any type of exception, but the garbage collector catches them, and so they have no effect.

Encapsulating explicit Java and third-party library exceptions

Using the Database class example from earlier on in this chapter, let us now look at how we could turn it into a full production model. In the chapter on encapsulation we suggested that you use packages to represent the "Facade" pattern and that is exactly what we are going to do here. Our Database class may be using JDBC and/or one or two other third-party packages. It would make our new database package really nasty for clients to use if we were to let exceptions thrown by the other class libraries we are using propagate out of the package. We have previously identified and defined the exception hierarchy so these will be the only exceptions thrown by methods in classes in our new package. So rather than forcing clients to understand the exceptions of the other class libraries involved, like this:

```
try
{
    db.open("emp_db");
}
catch(java.sql.SQLException ex) {...}
catch(thirdparty.SomeEx ex) {...}
```

they simply use our database package exceptions, making the package much easier to use:

```
catch(database.FatalDatabaseException ex) {...}
```

Incorrect usage of Java's exceptions

Just before we get stuck into some more advanced usages of exceptions we thought we should have a look at how not to use the Java exception mechanism.

Ill-conceived uses of exceptions that we have seen have included some bright spark who decided that he could return multiple types of objects from a method as follows – **do not do this!** A much more appropriate idiom for this type of behavior would be an Abstract Factory.

```
//DON'T USE EXCEPTIONS LIKE THIS
public class Factory
{
    static public void get(String type)
```

```
  {
    if(type.compareTo("Fish")==0)
      throw new Fish();
    //etc.
  }
}

public class Fish implements Throwable {...}
public class Dog implements Throwable {...}
//etc.

try
{
  Finder.get("Fish");
}
catch(Fish fish)   { /*got a fish back */}
catch(Dog dog)     { /*got a dog back */}
catch(Exception ex)
{
  //a real exception ????
}
```

So here is the rule:

Use exceptions to indicate exceptional and error conditions, *not* to return values from methods.

Need we say more?

Delegation-based exception handling

Imagine that the client end of our system has a GUI with many classes responsible for different views of the data. Each class uses a single shared instance of our Database class and is responsible for validating user input and invoking the appropriate methods on the Database instance, resulting in a design in which each method in each class implements an exceptions handler like those introduced earlier.

This idiom provides an alternative to the exception handling techniques described thus far. In the Delegation-based exception handling idiom an exception handler object is registered with a dispatcher object that is responsible for selecting the correct handler for the exception. If you think that this all sounds a bit like double dispatching, introduced in a previous chapter, you would be almost right. The reason behind this design decision is that we do not want to couple even an interface to our exception classes to allow them to be used either with this idiom or in a normal exception handling strategy.

The motivation behind this idiom is to delegate the exception handling of a known condition to a single handler, and it is particularly useful for handling exceptions from within threads (see the Callback idiom in Chapter 6) and in our GUI where status and error information has to be reported to the user. To make this example easier to understand we have focused on two DatabaseExceptions that could occur at any point in the program. They are the fatal condition of the database failing to open and the recoverable condition of failing to obtain a read lock on the requested objects. Previously we decided that if the database failed to open we would inform the user and then gracefully exit, whereas if we failed to obtain a read lock we would inform the user allowing them to try again later or continue with other options. The design of this idiom, as ever, relies on the use of a Java interface.

```
public interface ExHandler
{
  public void handleException(DatabaseException ex);
}
```

For this idiom to work we need to be able to have an exception handler for each type or category of exception, but without having to create too many more public classes. Fortunately inner classes solve our dilemma by letting a single public class contain more than one implementation of a single interface. To see how this works, examine carefully the test class below which provides implementations for two types of DatabaseException:

```
class DelegationExTest
{
  //impl...

  private class FatalErrorHandler
    implements ExHandler
  {
    public void handleException(DatabaseException ex)
    {
      System.out.println(ex.getMessage()+
            " system exiting...");
      System.exit(1);
    }
  }
  private class LockFailureHandler
    implements ExHandler
  {
    public void handleException(DatabaseException ex)
    {
      //report message to user
      //maybe in the status bar or dialog box?
    }
  }
}
```

Keep in mind that in the real world we would not choose to have a single class such as DelegationExTest handling both these types of exceptions – this just makes this idiom easier to explain.

Having defined the ExHandler interface and an implementation for two exception types, let us take a look at how to implement the dispatcher class.

```
public class ExCmdDispatcher
{
  private Hashtable cmds_ = new Hashtable();
  private ExHandler defhandler_;

  public ExCmdDispatcher(ExHandler def)
  {
    defhandler_=def;
  }

  public void addHandler(DbFault err,ExHandler cmd)
  {
    cmds_.put(err,cmd);
  }
  public void executeCmd(DatabaseException ex)
  {
    ExHandler handler=(ExHandler)cmds_.get(ex.getReasonCode());
    if(handler==null)
      defhandler_.handleException(ex);
    else
      handler.handleException(ex);

  }
}
```

If you take a closer look at ExCmdDispatcher you will see that it uses a Hashtable as a map between the reason code and the implementing class. This works initially by registering a typesafe constant key, along with a reference to an object implementing the ExHandler interface, then when executeCmd() is invoked with a DatabaseException object the method uses the Hashtable instance to return the ExHandler object associated with the DatabaseException reason code – easy, huh?

A final point to note about ExCmdDispatcher is that its constructor takes an ExHandler argument which will act as the default handler for exceptions not explicitly registered. The next section of code shows how you register your exception handlers; again we have included the code in our test class for clarity.

```
class DefaultExHandler
  implements ExHandler
{...}

class DelegationExTest
{
  private ExCmdDispatcher exdispatch_=new
    ExCmdDispatcher( new DefaultExHandler() );
```

```
public DelegationExTest()
{
  //registering inner classes...
  exdispatch_.addHandler(DbFault.DB_OPEN_ERROR,
    new FatalErrorHandler() );

  exdispatch_.addHandler(DbFault.READ_LOCK_FAILED,
    new LockFailureHandler() );
}
//as above
}
```

The class ExCmdDispatcher is a prime candidate for a Singleton which we will discuss in a later chapter. Finally we will add a method to our test class so you can see this idiom in action.

```
class DelegationExTest
{
  //as above
  public Enumeration testGetEmployees(Database db,String filter)
  {
    Enumeration emps=null
    try
    {
      emps = db.getEmployees(filter);
    }
    catch(DatabaseException ex)
    {
      //control transfers to either the inner class
      //FatalErrorHandler. HandleException( ex )
      //or LockFailureHandler
      //depending on the type of DatabaseException
      exdispatch_.executeCmd( ex );
    }
    return emps; //null on failure can be ignored
  }
}
```

Unfortunately our example does not really illustrate the full power of this idiom; to do so we would have had to include the code for a full GUI. However, if you imagine replacing all your duplicate exception handling code with a simple call to the dispatcher object you will begin to see the potential usage for this idiom, especially if the action resulting from the exception is to provide some feedback to the user via a shared component such as a status bar. By using this idiom, only the ExHandler implementation needs to know how to handle the exception and maintain a reference to, say, the status bar.

SUMMARY

In this chapter we have examined the classical approach to error handling and exposed some of its weaknesses. We have introduced many design principles in this chapter, which, if followed, can help you avoid some of the holes we fell into while developing our early Java systems.

Considering the types of exceptions that your system may generate, during the design phase, will go a long way to reducing its overall complexity. Delegated exception handling, or rethrowing exceptions, can be used effectively to handle exceptions that occur in threads or as an alternative approach to letting exceptions simply propagate up the call stack.

Java's exception mechanism is extremely powerful and can help you write more robust systems, so if you have not already started to incorporate exceptions into your own designs, now is the time.

6 Using callbacks

Polling in detail

Participants in callbacks

Implementing callbacks

Multicast callbacks

Handling exceptions with callbacks

Introduction

Consider the following scenario. You telephone a company's complaints department and ask to speak to the customer services manager. The likely response is "I'm sorry, Mr or Mrs... is busy right now." At this point there are three possible courses of action:

- Try again later.
- Hold the line and wait.
- Leave your phone number.

These actions have equivalents in the world of software engineering.

If you hang up and then keep recalling until you get to speak to the person in question, this is analogous to "polling" in software terminology. However, if you choose to hold the line your action is equivalent to a synchronous method call. Alternatively, if you leave your number, hang up and carry on with your normal daily routine, the phone may ring later in the day, your call being returned – this is a real-world example of a basic callback.

In software terms a callback is usually an asynchronous operation in which a client registers an interest in a particular event, or set of circumstances, and then carries on with its normal set of operations. If this event or set of circumstances occurs the client will be "interrupted" asynchronously, hence called back. For example, a GUI component in a trading system front-end may register with an object that is monitoring stocks and ask to be notified if a stock price goes above or below a particular level.

Before looking at callbacks in detail it is interesting to consider the other two actions above.

Synchronous method calls are the standard way in which methods are invoked in Java. Once a method has been invoked, the calling code blocks until either an exception is thrown or the method returns normally.

"Polling" describes a situation in which a client repeatedly, usually in a loop, invokes a method on another object to see if anything has changed.

Polling in detail

Using the stock example above, you may be tempted to write a polling version as follows. Pay close attention to the run() method in StockClient which "polls" the StockServer for the current value of the stock "ACME:EUR" and consider the implications if there are multiple StockClients all polling the StockServer.

```
public class StockServer
{
  public synchronized double getValue(String stockName)
  {...}
}

public class StockClient
  implements Runnable
{
  private double lowerLimit_;
  private double upperLimit_;
  private StockServer stockServer_;
  private boolean active_=true;

  public StockClient(StockServer srv,double lower,double upper)
  {
    stockServer_=srv;
    lowerLimit_=lower;
    upperLimit_=upper;
  }
  public void run()
  {
    while(active_)
    {
      double val=stockServer_.getValue("ACME:EUR");
      if(val<lowerLimit_ || val>upperLimit_)
      {
        //act on value being out of range
      }
    }
  }
}
```

The main problem with this design is that the server object StockServer will soon become overloaded with multiple client requests waiting for the object lock on the synchronized method getValue(). This design is also extremely inefficient and expensive in terms of system resources as each `StockClient` is executing in its own thread.

Other examples in which polling causes problems include clients re-executing a query on a set of objects in a database to make sure an up-to-date version of these objects is always being used. Generally this is a bad idea; not only are database queries usually resource intensive, but if many different clients are all interested in the same set of objects, and all using polling, the chance of actually obtaining the lock type you require on the objects is reduced significantly.

Database vendors have been wise to this problem for a long time and offer solutions such as triggers in relational databases and event notification in object database management systems. These are the database management systems' implementations of callbacks.

Participants in callbacks

There are two participants used to implement the callback idiom: the Caller, also known as the client, and the Receiver, also known as the server, which is responsible for performing the callback to the Caller when the correct set of circumstances occur. Generally the Receiver and Caller run in separate threads or processes, or there is little to be gained from this idiom.

It is kind of perverse – after the Caller has contacted the Receiver, the Caller becomes the Receiver and vice versa.

To summarize in pseudo code:

Caller to Receiver: "Let me know if x happens."
Caller carries on with its normal operations.
Some point later, Reciever to Caller: "x occurred."

The UML interaction diagram in Figure 6.1 shows the participants in action.

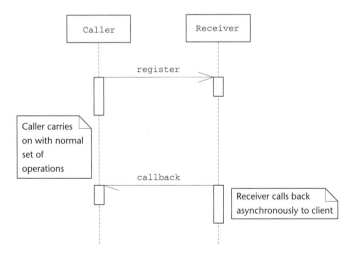

Figure 6.1 Generic callback idiom interaction diagram

Implementing callbacks

In some non-object-oriented programming languages callbacks are implemented by the client passing a "pointer to a function" to another server function. However, in Java we have a far more elegant and object-oriented mechanism – the interface. By using interfaces we can reduce the dependency between the participants in a design, in the case of callbacks between the Caller and the Receiver. Sticking with the stock server example above, we can redesign the classes as follows:

```
public interface StockListener
{
  public void valueChanged(double newValue);
}
```

The `StockListener` interface will be implemented by classes that want to act as stock listeners, that is, they want to be informed if a particular stock value changes. Their implementation of `valueChanged()` will be invoked by the new `StockServer` as a callback. So instead of `StockClient` implementing `Runnable` and polling the `StockServer`, we simply implement `StockListener`.

```
public class StockClient
  implements StockListener
{
  public void valueChanged(double newValue)
  {
    //act on new value
  }
}
```

Notice that the `StockClient` class is much smaller than before and that the dependency on class `StockServer` has been removed. The responsibility for monitoring the stock prices has now shifted to the `StockServer`.

```
public class StockServer extends Thread
{
  private StockListener stockListener_;
  private double lowerLimit_;
  private double upperLimit_;

  public void addStockListener(StockListener sl,
    String stock,double lower,double upper)
  {
    stockListener_=sl;
    lowerLimit_=lower;
    upperLimit_=upper;
  }

  public void run()
```

```
{
  while(true)
  {
    //monitor stock prices
    //update listener if stock has
    //moved out of range
    double newValue=0.0;
    //set to the new stock value then do the callback
    stockListener_.valueChanged( newValue );
  }
}
}
```

To see how this works, examine the sample client code below where a StockClient registers itself with the StockServer along with the stock it is interested in and the upper and lower limits. The method valueChanged() will be invoked as a callback on the registered StockClient if "ACME:EUR" goes below 109 or above 111.99.

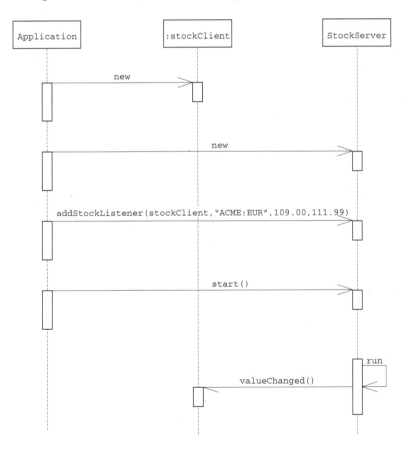

Figure 6.2 Stock example implementing callback idiom

```
StockClient stockClient= new StockClient();
StockServer srv= new StockServer();

srv.addListener(stockClient,"ACME:EUR",109.00,111.99);
srv.start(); //kick off server thread
```

The UML interaction diagram in Figure 6.2 shows the different participants interact.

Although our new stock system design is an improvement on the previous version which used a polling strategy, it is currently limited to a single StockListener. This type of one-to-one callback is often referred to as a *unicast callback*. To make our new stock system useful we need to use a *multicast callback* strategy.

Multicast callbacks

A multicast callback represents a one-to-many relationship for the callback idiom. To implement a multicast callback we need a mechanism to register multiple clients. For our stock system we can update the StockServer class to handle multiple clients, but for this strategy to be useful we also need a mechanism for de-registering clients. As we have used a Java interface and removed the coupling between StockClient and StockServer, the StockClient remains unaltered and would not require recompilation after the updates to StockServer. We have also encapsulated the modifications to StockServer so as not to impact any client classes that use the addStockListener() method. To achieve this we have used a new class to wrap the parameters to the addStockListener() method and act as a helper. If we had the luxury of completely rewriting all the classes involved we would have chosen to introduce an abstract class that implements StockListener and encapsulates the state and behavior we have introduced into SLHolder. However, in this case we are simply illustrating another example of encapsulation.

A UML class diagram for the multicast StockServer is shown in Figure 6.3.

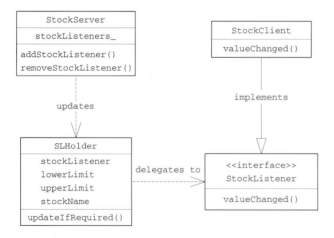

Figure 6.3 Stock classes implementing multicast callbacks

```
//wrapper for StockListener

class SLHolder
{
  private StockListener stockListener_;
  private String stockName_;
  private double lowerLimit_;
  private double upperLimit_;

  public SLHolder(StockListener sl,String stock,
      double lower,double upper)
  {
    stockListener_=sl;
    stockName_=stock;
    lowerLimit_=lower;
    upperLimit_=upper;
  }
  //helper method to reduce multiple getxxx()
  public void updateIfRequired(String stock,double val)
  {
    if(stockName_.equals(stock)
      && val<lowerLimit_ || val>upperLimit_)
    {
      //perform callback
      stockListener_.valueChanged( val );
    }
  }
  public StockListener getListener()
  { return stockListener_;}
}
```

Here is the updated code for the StockServer:

```
public class StockServer extends Thread
{
  private Hashtable stockListeners_ = new Hashtable();

  //updated server methods to register/de-register
  public synchronized
    void addStockListener(StockListener sl,
      String stock,double lower,double higher)
  {
    SLHolder slh=new SLHolder(sl,stock,lower,higher);

    //store in hash table with StockListener as key
    stockListeners_.put(sl,slh);
  }
```

```
public synchronized void removeListener(StockListener sl)
{
    //remove from hashtable
    stockListeners_.remove( sl );
}
//server thread
public void run()
{
    String stockName=null;
    double newvalue=0.0;

    while(true)
    {
        double newValue=0.0;
        //if some stock has changed
        //assign to stockName and newValue
        //see if any listeners are interested
        synchronized(stockListeners_)
        {
            Enumeration iter= stockListeners_.elements();
            while(iter.hasMoreElements())
            {
                SLHolder slh=(SLHolder)iter.nextElement();
                //delegate to helper class
                slh.updateIfRequired(stockName, newValue );
            }
        }
    }
}
}
```

The design for multicast callbacks is more complicated as we have to consider synchronizing access to the stockListeners_ Hashtable. The introduction of the helper class SLHolder moves some of the responsibility out of StockServer.run(), reducing the need to invoke multiple get methods on instances of SLHolder. Figure 6.4 shows the interaction diagram for the update stock system. Keep in mind that after start() is invoked on StockServer, asynchronous invocations can occur on addStockListener() and removeStockListener(), hence the need to synchronize both these methods and access to stockListeners_ in StockServer.run().

Also note how responsibility for invoking the callback has shifted to SLHolder.

By the way, we could have taken an alternative approach to specifying a method such as addStockListener() as synchronized by explicitly placing the synchronization around the critical section of the code as follows:

```
public void addStockListener(StockListener sl,
    String stock,double lower,double higher)
{
    SLHolder slh=new SLHolder(sl,stock,lower,higher);
```

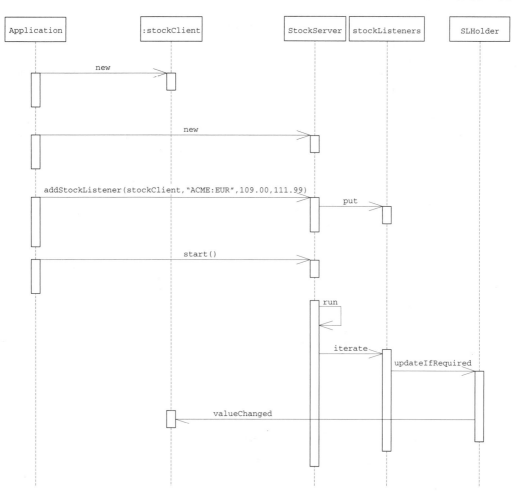

Figure 6.4 Multicast stock server interaction diagram

```
//critical section
synchronize(stockListeners)
{
    stockListeners_.put(sl,slh);
}
}
```

Up until now we have concerned ourselves with how to improve the stock system so it is more efficient and flexible, by switching from a polling strategy to a multicast callback strategy. There is one final area you need to consider when using the callback idiom – what to do if an exception occurs in the server. For example, our stock system would not be much use if the server crashed and clients did not know about it. To the end user of such a system the net result would appear as if the stock market had taken an extended break, as no prices would get updated!

Handling exceptions with callbacks

In the previous chapter we examined how to use delegated exception handling in a synchronous architecture. However, the full power of the delegated exception handling idiom becomes apparent with asynchronous architectures like our multicast stock server.

Delegated exception handling can be designed into a system using callbacks by adding additional method signatures to the callback interface. In the case of our StockListener we can simply declare another method as follows:

```
interface StockListener
{
  public void valueChanged(double newValue);
  public void serverException(String reason);
}
```

To keep the example simple, the new method serverException() will be invoked with a String parameter. In more advanced architectures the actual Exception object would be passed as a parameter. Here is the updated StockClient class:

```
public class StockClient
  implements StockListener
{
  public void valueChanged(double newValue)
  {
    //act on new value
  }
  public void serverException(String reason)
  {
    //act on server exception
    //notify users
  }
}
```

Finally, here is an example of how the StockServer could notify all listeners that an exception has occurred. In this example the exception is assumed to be fatal, so all listeners are notified and the thread exits. However, other designs would distinguish between fatal and recoverable exceptions and employ different strategies to handle these.

```
//StockServer run()

public void run()
{
  try
  {
    //as before
  }
```

```
catch(ServerException ex) //defined elsewhere
{
  synchronized(stockListeners_)
  {
    Enumeration iter= stockListeners_.elements();
    while(iter.hasMoreElements())
    {
      SLHolder slh=(SLHolder)iter.nextElement();
      //pass to helper class
      StockListener sl=slh.getListener();
      //notify listener of exception
      sl.serverException(ex.getMessage());
    }
  }
}
}
```

SUMMARY

The callback idiom is extremely powerful and underlies many other idioms and patterns. The Observer pattern uses a multicast callback to notify Observers if an Observable has changed. In fact our StockServer is implementing an Observer/ Observable model and could easily be updated to use the Java interface Observer and Observable class to implement our design.

Java 1.1.x introduced the delegated event model for the AWT; this too is implemented as a multicast callback. In this case multicasting is implemented in a chaining model via an AWTEventMulticaster, which is another interesting twist on this idiom.

The callback idiom becomes increasingly powerful when systems become distributed. Polling a local server is bad enough, but when polling occurs across low bandwidth connections the problems outlined in this chapter become even more critical, and do not even think about a blocking strategy for lengthy operations.

Be careful to consider synchronization and multiple threading issues, and also exception handling, when using this idiom.

7 Loading classes and creating objects

Loading classes

Creating objects

Using dynamic class loading

Using objects and classes

Reachability

Object removal

Finalize

Class unloading

Introduction

Understanding how Java loads classes and creates objects is key to using the Java environment in an efficient and elegant way.

The Java language and virtual machine support the ability to load classes dynamically at runtime. This feature is generally not present in programming languages that are compiled into platform-specific executables. In these languages, functions or methods are statically linked into the program, so once you have compiled and linked the program you are committed to those implementations. Dynamic link libraries offer some flexibility, but again these libraries themselves must be compiled and statically linked.

Every object in Java has an associated class or type; this is the object's Class class. By using this information, we can find out the type of any particular object at runtime – and as we saw earlier, this is key to the polymorphism mechanism in Java. This means that before we can create an object of a particular type, or use the static methods or fields of a class, we must load the class information into a Class class.

Before we can discuss the creation of objects we also need to discuss the way that classes are loaded into the Java runtime. So really this chapter is about two lifetimes.

The outer or enclosing lifetime is that of the Class class. The start of this lifetime is the time at which the class is loaded and the end of this lifetime is the time at which the class is unloaded or the runtime that contains the class is stopped.

The second or inner lifetime is the lifetime of an object created from a particular class. An object's life starts when it is created, and ends when the object is no longer useful.

Unlike some other languages, once an object is no longer useful it is the responsibility of the Java runtime to dispose of it, not the Java programmer.

Loading classes

Under normal circumstances programmers and users are unaware of classes being loaded because the JVM automatically loads classes behind the scenes.

Automatic class loading happens in one of two ways. Either a static method or instance field is accessed on a class requiring the class-based information to be loaded, or an object instance of a previously unreferenced class is created via the use of the new keyword. In order to create any new object, the class information is required, and so the class must be loaded before the object can be created. In this case the resulting object would be the first instance of this newly loaded class.

```
//SineWave has not been used before
//SineWave class is not loaded.

SineWave wave = new SineWave(); // SineWave class is now loaded.
```

When a class is loaded the Java runtime is required to run any static initializers that have been declared in the class. This can take the form of initializing any static member fields or one or a number of static initializer blocks, generally one. In the following example both member field initialization and a static initializer block are used.

```java
public class SineWave
{
  private final static int WAVE_SAMPLES = 100;
  private static float [] waveTable = new float[WAVE_SAMPLES];

  static
  {
    // populate the wave table at load time
    final double HALF_WAVE = Math.PI / 2.0;
    final double increment = HALF_WAVE/WAVE_SAMPLES;
    double angle = 0.0;
    for (int i = 0; i < WAVE_SAMPLES; i++)
    {
      // may load Math class on first iteration
      waveTable[i] = (float)Math.sin(angle);
      angle += increment;
    }
  }

  // ... remainder of the class ...
}
```

In this case the SineWave class is creating a lookup table when it is loaded in order to store the values that are retrieved when calling the sin() method available in the java.lang.Math class. If the Math class had not been referenced before the call to the static sin() method, this would force the Math class to be loaded as a side effect of calling the method. Precalculating values like this and storing them in a lookup table is an old graphics programmers' trick which is intended to make finding values for particular mathematical functions faster. Static initializers lend themselves to this type of preloading of static information shared by any number of instances of a class. However, like any performance enhancing trick, you may find that this works well in some circumstances but it is not beneficial in others.

It is possible to define a number of static initializer blocks, but again the more complex and coupled the activity of the initializer block is, the more likely we are to trip ourselves up. As ever, it is important to have a clearly and simply defined role for the initializer that deals with a set of localized fields. Even in this case beware of weird "order of intialization" problems. There are some well-defined rules for the behavior of static initializers that you can find in the language specification, so if you are doing anything non-trivial in this area it is best to check the spec thoroughly.

As we have seen, a class gets loaded into the runtime environment when it is required. This makes a lot of sense in most cases and in special cases such as exceptions it can save a lot of unnecessary load time. If we make the assumption that in general an exception is not going to be thrown by a system, it does not make sense to load the exception class unless it is required. In some cases we can imagine a system that may run for number of years and never loads and throws particular exceptions.

At the other end of the spectrum, dynamic class loading can be very noticeable in the case of applets that have been loaded over the Internet via HTTP for example. If you have ever wondered why there is a delay sometimes when your applets use classes that reside on the server and that need to be downloaded for the first time, it is often that the class is being dynamically loaded and the delay is due to the class being transmitted from the server. This often happens when you open new frames that make use of previously unreferenced classes. Packaging commonly referenced classes in a JAR file can prevent this problem in some cases, but again it is not always possible to know which classes will be referenced by an applet or application.

So occasionally it may be useful to force the JVM to load a class. This can be done in a number of ways. Two common and generally applicable ways are either to use the static method forName on the class Class:

```
Class c1 =Class.forName("java.lang.String");
```

or, since JDK 1.1 using a Class literal:

```
Class c1=java.lang.String.class;
```

In both cases, in order to set the reference to the class c1 the JVM/ClassLoader will first check that the class has not already been loaded. If it has, the current ClassLoader will return a reference to the existing class object, otherwise the ClassLoader will attempt to load it, and then fix up the reference to the class and return it.

Getting nearer to the machine, you can ask the ClassLoader object to load the class directly by calling the loadClass() method that is defined in the ClassLoader interface. Applying the limbo principle – only go as low as you need to – it is better to use the higher-level methods wherever possible, because directly manipulating system-level objects can result in unexpected effects, unless your code is extremely tidy and well behaved within the particular programming context.

Creating objects

From the Java applications programmer's perspective, objects may be created in one of two simple ways. One is the direct use of the new keyword like this:

```
SineWave wave = new SineWave();
```

As we have seen, this will force the class SineWave to be loaded if it is not already present and then an object of the type SineWave will be created for us.

The main alternative is to create a new instance by using the newInstance() method on a class's Class object to construct the new object. This technique has the limitation that it is only possible to create the object by a call to the default constructor. If you want access to non-default constructors it is necessary to use the reflection mechanism which goes beyond the scope of this book, but is none the less an interesting area for investigation.

In both of these main cases, when a new object is created we can see the process of construction as a set of operations. First of all the memory is allocated to store the new instance of the class; following this the constructor of the class is invoked. Once the constructor has run, the reference to the object is returned to the client code – this is why constructors are special in that although no return type is allowed to be specified, the return type is always, in effect, a reference to the new object of the type of the class.

So far this is a relatively simple process; however, things start to get a little more complex when we introduce the idioms of constructor chaining, inheritance, or both.

Constructor chaining is where a number of constructors are defined for the same class, and in order to prevent the repetition of code or replacement of values, one constructor calls the code in another. Here is an example of constructor chaining using the this keyword in the form of a method call:

```
public class PlacedShape
{
    private int x_;
    private int y_;
    private Shape shape_;

    public PlacedShape()
    {
        this(1,1);
    }

    public PlacedShape(int x, int y)
    {
        this(x,y, new Shape());
    }
```

```
public PlacedShape(int x, int y, Shape shape)
{
    x_ = x;
    y_ = y;
    shape_ = shape;
}
}
```

This form is extremely robust in the face of changes because it localizes the actual setting of parameters to a single constructor, at the expense of a number of constructor calls to implement the simpler constructors.

> **P** Use constructor chaining to make constructor behaviour and default values appear in only one place in the chain.

In the case of inheritance it is necessary to use the similar form, but with super to "call up" to the parent class of the object before initializing this class; of course, this is only necessary when we want to call a constructor in the parent class that is not the default constructor, or the default constructor is not available. This form is extremely common in the area of exception classes.

```
class EndOfCakeException extends Exception
{
  public EndOfCakeException()
  { super("Still hungry at end of Cake"); }
  public EndOfCakeException(String reason)
  { super(reason); }
}
```

All of the code above conforms to the Java rules that calls to super or this must appear first in the body of the constructor code. However, in a case where we want to use constructor chaining via this, but we have also extended another class containing explicit constructors, both calls cannot appear first. The example below illustrates the potential problem:

```
public class BoundedPlacedShape extends PlacedShape
{
  private Constraints constraints_;

  public BoundedPlacedShape(Constraints c)
  {
    constraints_=c;
  }

  public BoundedPlacedShape(Constraints c,int x, int y)
  {
    super(x,y); // must be first call in constructor
    this(c);    // must be first call in constructor
  }
}
```

This may look like a major problem in that the call to super() and the call to this() must both be the first call in a constructor. However, by carefully designing your classes as follows, you can easily avoid what appears to be a no-win situation.

(P) Use private helper methods to avoid super() and this() conflicts in constructor chaining.

Possibly the simplest approach to avoiding this problem is to introduce a private init() method. We use init() to be short for initialization – not to be confused with the JVM-level <init> methods. So now we can use method delegation to factor out our common constructor code and solve the problem.

```
public class BoundedPlacedShape extends PlacedShape
{
  private Constraints constraints_;

  public BoundedPlacedShape(Constraints c)
  {
    init(c); // delegate to init method
  }

  public BoundedPlacedShape(Constraints c,int x, int y)
  {
    super(x,y);
    init(c);
  }
  private void init(Constraints c) // ctor helper method
  {
    constraints_=c;
  }
}
```

Again this brings us back to one of our very first idioms of method delegation – moving common code out into another method and then calling that method in order to do the work. In this case we have moved the shared constructor behavior out into a new method – the constructor helper init() – to avoid the necessity of constructor chaining, and of course we gain the other benefits derived from this idiom in the cases where we have used it before.

While we are on the subject of constructors and init() methods, it is worth taking a look at some of the problems you may encounter when using constructors with abstract classes. It may not at first appear to make sense to define a constructor in an abstract class. Remember that abstract classes cannot be instantiated by any explicit method. That means that an abstract class can only exist as a "part" of a concrete class within a class hierarchy. However, this does not mean that the constructor for the abstract class will not get called at all; indeed it may well get called by an implicit or explicit use of the super keyword from a child class's constructor.

Let us look at some code for a "laser" shooting game which involves shooting at a sequence of moving targets. We have defined the abstract class Mover which has a constructor and an abstract method advance() which forces any child class to implement this method and then specify a way to move that is appropriate for any class that is extending it.

```
abstract class Mover
{
  public Mover()
  {
    System.out.println( "MoverConstructor");
    //as soon as something is constructed start moving it
    advance(); //invoke abstract method.
  }

    abstract public void advance(); //all movers must advance
}
```

Here is a target class for the shooting game which extends Mover, giving us a MovingTarget:

```
public class MovingTarget extends Mover
{
  private int position_ = 0; //for clarity

  public MovingTarget(int position)
  {
    System.out.println( "Setting position to :" + position);
    position_ = position;
  }

  public void advance()
  {
    position_ += 1; //for simplicity
    System.out.println( "Advance: Position is " + position_);
  }
}
```

Now this is completely legal code – try it in your compiler – but the result of the output is not what we may expect. Code like this:

```
MovingTarget mt = new MovingTarget(100);
```

produces output like this:

```
MoverConstructor:
Advance: Position is 1
Setting position to 100
```

This is because we are mixing object creation with object usage. In other words, we are using the object's methods before we have finished using its constructors. To avoid falling down this hole in future, let us make a general rule:

(T)   Never call an abstract method from a constructor in an abstract class.

There are many ways of unbundling this problem but the key thing to remember is to not mix constructors and abstract methods in constructor chains. If you cannot initialize an object into the state that you require via the constructor path, it is generally far simpler and more "state safe" to use an init() method that completes the concrete or abstract initialization via methods, as we saw earlier.

There are some compiler rules that come to our aid and prevent too much mayhem in this area. Just so that this rule sticks in your mind, here is a quirky example:

```
class Cake extends Food
{
  public Cake ()
  {
    super(eat()); // == super(this.eat());
  }
  public int eat()
  {
    // eat the cake
  }
}
```

This is illegal because of the implicit use of this in the call to eat(). Anyway, the mere thought of a cake that eats itself before it has been made is a little too surreal even for us to contemplate!

Using dynamic class loading

Now that we have looked at class loading and object creation it is interesting to see how we can combine our knowledge of these features using the example of a simple language translator that is intended to translate single words of English into other languages.

A couple of things to keep in mind before we go any further:

*   You can only create new instances of a class through newInstance() if that class has a default constructor. If the class does not have a public default constructor, newInstance() will throw a NoSuchMethodError.

*   newInstance() only works for concrete classes, that is, it will not work for abstract classes or interfaces.

For our example language translator, the requirements state that the system should be flexible enough to support many different languages, some of which will not be known at the time that we develop the initial product.

To keep the example simple, the class UniversalTranslator's main() method takes two arguments, the first being the word to be translated and the second specifying the class name of the concrete translator. This example uses both class.forName() for dynamic loading and polymorphism in the form of the call to translateWord().

```
class WordNotFoundException extends Exception
{
  public WordNotFoundException(String why) {super(why);}
}

interface Translator
{
  public String translateWord(String word)
    throws WordNotFoundException;
}

class FrenchTranslator implements Translator
{
  public String translateWord(String word)
    throws WordNotFoundException
  {
    System.out.println("FrenchTranslator.translateWord()");
    //lookup word and return or throw exception ...
    throw new WordNotFoundException(word);
  }
}

public class UniversalTranslator
{
  static public void main(String [] args)
  {
    try
    {
      Class c=Class.forName(args[1]);
      Translator t=(Translator)c.newInstance();
      t.translateWord(args[0]);
    }
    //for brevity - generally don't catch Exception
    catch(Exception ex)
    {
      ex.printStackTrace();
    }
  }
}
```

So to translate the English word Hello into French we would use the following command line to produce the following output.

```
>java UniversalTranslator Hello FrenchTranslator
FrenchTranslator.translateWord()
Bonjour
```

So this appears to work fine and we have class structure that can cope with the addition of further languages. Just for fun we could define a KlingonTranslator to prove the point and pass it as a command line argument as before:

```
class KlingonTranslator implements Translator
{
  public String translateWord(String word)
    throws WordNotFoundException
  {
    System.out.println("KlingonTranslator.translateWord()");
    //lookup word and return or throw exception ...
    throw new WordNotFoundException(word);
  }
}
```

For the sake of comparison, let us take a step back for a moment and imagine that we have to re-implement UniversalTranslator without using the facility of dynamic class loading. One approach might be to check the second parameter given to the application, the translator type, and then instantiate the appropriate concrete translator in the UniversalTranslator as follows:

```
Translator t=null;
if(args[1].equals("FrenchTranslator"))
  t= new FrenchTranslator();
if(args[1].equals("KlingonTranslator"))
  t= new KlingonTranslator();

// ... etc., etc. ...
if (t != null ) t.translateWord(args[0]);
```

The problem with this code is that in taking this step back we have ended up where we started in our discussion on polymorphism. The context here is different, but the principle remains the same – switch constructs or chained if–else clauses are not only a nightmare to maintain, but should not be used to determine runtime behavior. Another potential problem with this second approach is that class UniversalTranslator, or some other class in the program, has to know about all the possible concrete types of translators.

Using the dynamic class loading approach, new classes can be added without recompilation. In fact we could even provide a third party with the Translator interface, who in turn could supply us with compiled class files for other language translators, thus extending one of the original requirements. As long as the other party implemented the Translator properly according to our Translator interface, all we would have to do is ship their .class files along with our own, or even dynamically load them via HTTP from their Web site. So in our rather simplistic example we could then use the following command line, assuming that this class is accessible via the class path:

```
>java UniversalTranslator hello thirdparty.JavaneseTranslator
```

So we can use dynamic class loading to implement a truly global "plug and play" component infrastructure for our translation system, in which third parties can supply their own components without our knowledge so long as they subscribe properly to the Translator's interface.

Using objects and classes

The second phase of an object's lifetime is its use. We are already extremely familiar with this model in which we use a live object reference to access the methods of objects that we – or others – have constructed. By convention we have decided that the only way we are going to use objects and classes is by calling methods on them – with the exception of using static final fields as constant values.

You might like to check some of the earlier chapters if some of this is not obvious to you, but by way of a swift review, let us look a little more deeply at what is happening when we invoke either class- or object-based methods.

```
public class MethodTest
{
   static public void classMethod() {}
   public void instanceMethod() {}
}
```

Class methods are those declared as static and do not require an object instance in order to be invoked. static methods and static fields are referred to as belonging to a class rather than an instance of that class. We know that class names have to be unique, so we can use this knowledge to conclude that there will only ever be one instance of a static method (it cannot be overridden) or field for a specific use of a class. This means that a single copy of the field is shared by all instances of that class.

Using the example above we can invoke classMethod() without having to create an instance of the class MethodTest:

```
MethodTest.classMethod();
```

When your Java compiler encounters code like this it can determine the runtime type MethodTest and generate an invokestatic byte code instruction for that class method – this is known as static binding. This is reasonably straightforward and effectively the same process used by compilers for languages without dynamic binding. Let us now consider what the compiler does when it encounters an instance method.

Using the above example class, as written, if the Java compiler encounters a method in some other class that takes a MethodTest instance as a parameter it has no way to determine at compile time whether the runtime type of the parameter is of the declared type or one of its subclasses – unless of course MethodTest or the method being invoked is declared as a final.

```
public void otherClassMethod(MethodTest mt)
{
  //mt could be an instance of MethodTest
  //or any of its subclasses
  mt.instanceMethod();
}
```

So what is the compiler going to do here?

If the method being invoked is declared `final` in the class of the object instance, the compiler can determine the method to invoke and can generate an `invokenonvirtual` byte code instruction. In our example `instanceMethod()` is not declared `final`, thus the compiler cannot determine the runtime type of the parameter `mt`, as it could be a subclass of `MethodTypes` which overrides `instanceMethod()`. Under these circumstances the compiler will generate an `invokevirtual` byte code instruction, which defers finding the correct method to invoke to the Java runtime – this is dynamic binding. Invoking *virtual* methods is the way that the JVM implements type-dependent behavior at runtime as we described in the chapter on polymorphism.

Reachability

Once a reference to an object being created has been returned, the object is termed reachable, meaning that at least one other client object has a reference to this "live" object. When a variable is referencing a valid object, we can also say that the object is reachable. The idea of reachability is powerful because when an object is no longer reachable – that is, there are no valid references to it held by other objects or classes – the Java runtime can make the assumption that the object is no longer useful within the system. However, certain idioms in Java, most notably the Singleton, are not reachable in certain conditions although they remain useful objects. We will look at this idiom more closely in the next chapter.

However, we can generally state that if an object becomes unreachable from the client code, in almost all cases it is safe to assume that the object is no longer of use and so it is ready to be removed from the runtime system.

Object removal

Part of the amazing power of Java and its high productivity gains derives from the fact that the Java runtime takes responsibility for removing objects that are no longer useful.

However, because the Java runtime takes this responsibility it has to make some assumptions about the environment, and implement quite a complex procedure to deal with a number of boundary cases. Object removal is performed by the eloquently and descriptively named garbage collector (GC).

Various theories and methods have become a very hot topic in the area of garbage collection since Java has taken off, and much of the work done in making SmallTalk, for example, efficient in this area is being reused and taken to new heights through research and development efforts.

When an object is no longer useful to a client program it is a good idea to mark that object, as a hint to the garbage collector, by setting the object reference to null.

```
// make a wave
SineWave wave = new SineWave();

// ... use the wave ...

// wave is no longer useful so make
// it unreachable from this ref.

wave = null;
```

The garbage collector's job is now made simpler because it is easier to work out that the object is no longer reachable, given of course that a reference is not held to the object in another part of the program. However, this does not mean that the object has been removed or indeed that it ever will be! It is just a hint to the GC that the object is no longer useful to the client code.

This is the place where things start to get a little fuzzy unless we introduce a clearer model of the process of object removal. It is as if the object has reached a point where it is neither alive nor active to the client code, but the runtime may still make calls on the object (e.g. finalize) and it still exists in local memory. At this point objects are in a kind of Java purgatory, dead as far as the program is concerned, but not fully purged!

So what guarantees does the Java runtime make that the object will be collected and put out of its half-dead misery? Well, the short answer is none; this can be a little hard to cope with, especially in safety-critical and embedded systems, but in most cases, once you get used to it, it makes life far simpler, given the advantage that it is no longer necessary to care about explicitly removing objects in client code.

Finalize

As well as constructors, objects may also implement a finalize method. Finalize methods are very useful for closing down resources that have been opened by methods that are generally only called once, such as constructors and some init methods.

As an example, here is some code that opens a video stream from a video camera node in a constructor, and uses finalize to close down the node when it is no longer required.

```
public class LiveVideoStream
{
  private VideoNode node_;

  public LiveVideoStream()
  {
    node_ = new VideoNode(VideoNode.MPEG2);
  }
```

```
//other methods

public void finalize()
  throws Throwable //declared in Object.finalize()
{
  node_.close();
  //be a good citizen of the class hierarchy
  super.finalize();
}

}
```

Notice the careful use of the call to super.finalize() in the example above. This is necessary because the Java runtime will only call finalize() on the instantiated type of object, not every finalize() method in a class hierarchy. Given that we must call super as the first call of a constructor, we can use the symmetry to give us a new Java rule.

(R) Always call super.finalize() at the end of a finalize() method.

However, it is really important to keep in mind that finalize() methods are not simply a reversal of the behavior of constructors, as destructors are in C++. So we cannot always use this symmetrical property as a way of solving problems with finalizers; for example there is no such thing as a default finalizer, and so it is possible to "catch a crab" by blindly applying this symmetrical approach. It may be useful in suggesting a solution to some design situations, but it must be tempered by an understanding of the underlying behavior of the garbage collector and runtime system.

The Java runtime makes the guarantee that *it* will only call the finalize method once in the course of an object's lifetime, which looks like a benefit because it does not make sense to close the VideoNode twice. In fact, attempting to close some resources twice can result is some bizarre bugs occasionally appearing in systems. But remembering the other (non) guarantees made with respect to object removal means that it is possible (not probable) that the video node will never get closed and continue to consume resources in the Java runtime space.

In most cases this will be fine because if space becomes limited the GC will kick in and as a part of this process the finalize method will get called implicitly. However, it is possible to imagine a situation in which delivery throughput and resource management are key to the provision of certain services, such as the case of the video server. In such cases it may appear to make sense to call finalize() explicitly as soon as the node is no longer useful, but this is not the case.

(R) Never call finalize() explicitly.

Here is the method that is used by a client class to close the video stream:

```
public void closeVideoStream()
{
   //explicitly finalize the object, forcing the node to close
   videoStream.finalize(); //May get called again by JVM
   //hint to the gc that this object is no longer in use
   videoStream = null;
}
```

So now we are sure that the finalize() method has been called, but the GC/runtime may call the finalize() method again when the videoStream object is collected. Remember the guarantee was that the *runtime* would only call finalize() once. If we call finalize(), the runtime is still at liberty to call it later, thus re-executing the call to close the node and finalize() for the superclass.

In order to prevent this we can use a reverse of our trick for getting out of trouble with constructor chaining: we can introduce a method that can be called directly to release any resources but still use the finalize() method to perform a double check that the resources have been released.

So for our example LiveVideoStream class we define the following field and method to manage the releasing of resources:

```
private boolean released_ = false;

public synchronized void release()
{
   if (!released_)
   {
      node_.close();
      released_ = true;
   }
}

public void finalize()
   throws Throwable
{
   release();
   super.finalize();
}
```

Now our code for directly closing the video stream at a given time would look like this:

```
public void closeVideoStream()
{
   //explicitly release any resources
   videoStream.release();
   //hint to the gc that this object is no longer in use
   videoStream = null;
}
```

This code could be duplicated or run on other threads without risking any side effects of closing the node twice, and the `finalize()` method can be used to ensure that if a client has not called the release method, it will take on this responsibility. So any way around, the node is guaranteed to be released and released only once, by the time the object is garbage collected.

As a final note, in certain situations you may consider using the `System.run Finalization()` method which asks the Java runtime to invoke `finalize()` on all objects waiting in the finalization queue. Again there is no guarantee that the JVM will actually do this, so in critical situations always use a releaser method strategy.

Class unloading

Now that we have looked at the full life cycle for an object it is interesting to close this chapter by looking at class unloading, thus completing the runtime life cycle for a class.

It comes as a surprise to a number of Java programmers that it is possible for classes to be unloaded before an applet or application is terminated. This is normally a surprise because this behavior is not implemented in a number of JVMs. However, in server-side systems that are required to run for long periods, class unloading is necessary to prevent JVM memory filling up with unused classes and other class-based resources that are no longer required.

Classes may get unloaded when the `ClassLoader` that loaded them is no longer in use, but as in the case of objects, classes can only be unloaded when they are no longer in use or reachable by any other class or object in the system. We strongly recommend that you do not write your systems to depend on classes being unloaded, in any particular way, order, or at any specific time. It is advisable to check the current specifications for detailed class unloading information and to understand that this behavior may vary between different VMs.

In keeping with the object life cycle, there is a `classFinalize()` method that will be called by the runtime when the class is unloaded; generally this would be used for releasing resources used by the class, which may have been consumed by the static initializer block for the class. All of the principles that we have described for object finalizations may also be applied to class finalization as much the same basic rules apply.

SUMMARY

Before any object can be created, the class of that object must be loaded into the Java runtime. The lifetime of a class always contains all of the lifetimes of any objects that are created from it.

In normal circumstances classes are loaded automatically by a combination of the Java runtime and the `ClassLoader` object. When a class is loaded, static initializers are run, both field initializers and static initializer blocks.

It is possible to force the runtime to load classes that have not yet been referenced; this can be used to prevent programs "stalling" at runtime when new paths in the code are followed that require previously unreferenced classes to be loaded.

As the behavior of constructors becomes more complex, either through chaining, inheritance, or both, it may be worth considering delegating the constructor behavior to a `private init()` method defined for the class.

Dynamic class loading allows us to build flexible systems that may be modified by ourselves or third parties in the future without the need to rebuild our current systems, and without losing type safety.

When objects are no longer useful they are tidied away by the garbage collector. Garbage collection leads to a massive reduction of bugs and complexity at the client programmer level but the price we pay is a more complex runtime environment with a less determinable nature. Sometimes using a release strategy in conjunction with finalizers is appropriate in order to simplify object finalization and clean-up.

8 Creational idioms

Object factory

Factory method

Abstract Factory

Singleton

Singleton adapter

"Virtual" Constructor idiom

Introduction

The area of object creation occupies a special place in the world of design patterns and programming idioms. In the previous chapter we looked at how objects may be created explicitly via the use of the `new` keyword and the `newInstance()` method.

In this chapter we are going to take a look at ways of creating objects without directly calling constructors, and examine the design balances that have to be struck when using this approach. This can raise the degree of abstraction that we may use to design and code Java software, with all the inherent benefits that using higher levels of abstraction achieves. We aim to develop these ideas into some more sophisticated Java idioms and guide you through some of the techniques used for creating objects in more abstract ways.

The proposed solutions and alternatives we investigate in this chapter relate to the forces acting within the examples that we describe; however, we have tried to focus on recurring design issues relating to the idioms and patterns presented. As you work your way through this chapter please take time to consider carefully the design issues raised and how they may affect the project or system that you are currently working on, or how the solutions offered may have improved a previous project's design; these may vary subtly from the examples given.

Let us start by looking at a fundamental feature of many creational idioms – the object factory.

Object factory

The generic term "object factory" is analogous to a factory in the real world: it makes products, but of the object-oriented variety, not automobiles, CDs, or bars of soap.

Some people like to call factories "kits;" we suppose that it depends on your background. Whichever model you choose, in OO software design this equates to the factory taking responsibility for instantiating an object, as opposed to the client code.

For example, instead of the client code doing

```
Product p = new Product();
```

it would use a factory object in the form

```
Product p = factory.makeProduct();
```

where the factory instantiates an instance of class `Product` and returns it to the client.

Factory method

A number of patterns and Java idioms we introduce depend on the manipulation of an object via an interface. In essence the use of interfaces allows us to "plug and play" with various concrete objects behind an interface without affecting the client code. Well actually, it allows us to play, it is the plug that we are concerned with in this section.

When it comes to defining interfaces we know that they cannot specify constructors – there are a host of reasons – but above all it simply does not make any sense to define the creation time behavior of an object that you cannot create.

Also you cannot specify the constructors for all of the concrete implementors of an interface in the interface's method declarations. Even if you could, we would destroy any code maintenance benefits that we may have achieved so far. So although we can *virtualize* out all of the methods we cannot *virtualize* out the constructors by this means:

```
interface Node
{
  public VideoNode(); //not legal

  public void configure();
  //more method definitions
}
class VideoNode
  implements Node
{
  public VideoNode()
  { ... }
  //concrete methods
}
```

So we are left at the time of object creation with the job of having to specify the concrete type and referring to it through the interface.

```
Node outputNode = new VideoNode();
outputNode.configure();
```

In order to make the concrete type completely hidden we use the *factory method* idiom. There are several different variations on this theme and you will sometimes hear references to *virtual constructors*, which amount to much the same thing. Later on you will see how to write a *virtual* constructor that actually looks like a constructor and not a method!

For a factory method implementation we need to define an interface through which we can create a concrete object and return an abstract type:

```
interface NodeMaker
{
  Node makeNode(); //a method
}
```

and then make a concrete node maker:

```
class NodeMakerImpl
  implements NodeMaker
{
  Node makeNode()
  {
    return new VideoNode();
  }
}
```

so now we can completely remove the reference to the concrete class from the client source code:

```
NodeMaker noder = new NodeMakerImpl();
Node outputNode = noder.makeNode();
outputNode.configure();
```

Now we have removed from the client code any trace of the type of node that is created. In the single example above, there does not seem to be much benefit in using this idiom; however, we only need to apply the same arguments that we applied for originally motivating the need for interfaces to realize how powerful this idiom is. To illustrate this, consider the method below which is written in terms of the interfaces Node and NodeMaker rather than their concrete types VideoNode and NodeMakerImpl:

```
class NodeTester
{
  static void unitTest(NodeMaker noder)
  {
    Node outputNode = noder.makeNode();
    outputNode.configure();
    //run tests on outputNode ...
  }
}
```

- Creational idioms

```
//client code

NodeMaker noder = new NodeMakerImpl();
NodeTester.unitTest( noder );
```

Once again, by using interfaces we have "future proofed" our code. That is, if new concrete implementations of NodeMaker are introduced that return other types of Nodes we do not have to alter NodeTester.unitTest().

In fact at this stage we are at a really pivotal point on the route to a number of other more complex creational and related patterns. It is, if you can forgive the hyperbole, as if we are standing at the dawn of creation for a number of the further creational patterns and idioms. OK, maybe you cannot forgive us, but this really is the start of a large number of really interesting and useful idioms.

If we introduce a few new forces we can turn the factory method into a number of other idioms. For example, if we say that we want to group a number of related factory methods into a single interface to reduce the overhead of having a new class for every *virtualized* object that we want to make, we end up with an abstract factory or kit.

Or we may want to fold the *virtual* constructor back into the concrete class so that the class can make an instance or instances of itself! If we implement this as a static method on the class, we are well on the way to the Singleton idiom.

Both Abstract Factory and Singleton are described in depth later in this chapter.

After that brief diversion we are going to return to our VideoSystem by extending the example we developed earlier, towards a framework for serving various different types of digital content. The aim is that the framework has no knowledge of the types of nodes and digital content that is being sent to those nodes. Frameworks can be generated in a number of ways. In this case we are going to describe some classes for our Multi-Media framework which allows us to plug in new media types via the inheritance mechanism.

First of all we know that Nodes can be configured, they can be pushed some content, and they can be reset if they get out of sync, so we are going to record this in our Node interface:

```
interface Node
{
  public void configure();
  public void push(Content c);
  public void reset();
}
```

We make the ServerFramework responsible for containing nodes and defining a factory method for them but it does not know about specific node types and so cannot specifically create a node type. We are going to use inheritance to make specific servers that can handle various types of nodes:

```
abstract class ContentServer
{
  private Vector nodes_;
```

```
//... ctors etc.
//factory method to be overridden by 'actual' server
public abstract Node makeNode();

public void setUpNode()
{
  Node node = makeNode(); //invokes subclass impl
  node.configure();
  nodes_.addElement(node);
}

public void resetAllNodes()
{
  //loop over all nodes and call reset
}
//other concrete server methods
}
```

So we can now write generic and useful code in the framework which is going to help us when we create the concrete server. In this case, a video server:

```
class VideoServer extends ContentServer
{
  //ctors etc.

  //must define this
  public Node makeNode() //invoked from super.setUpNode()
  {
    return new VideoNode();
  }

  //other methods specific to the video server
}
```

To match the VideoServer we need to define the concrete node for Video:

```
class VideoNode implements Node
{
  public void configure()
  { /* impl */ }
  public void push(Content c)
  { /* impl */ }
  public void reset()
  { /* impl */ }
}
```

The UML diagram in Figure 8.1 shows how the framework is built around the abstract class ContentServer and the interface Node. This design allows us to develop an AudioServer, for example, or any other content type server into this framework

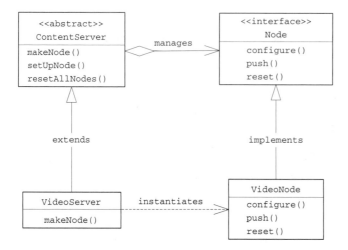

Figure 8.1   Content server class diagram

without a rewrite of the basic server code which resides in `ContentServer`. This is a relatively simple version of a framework that may be extended by inheritance into a more application specific area.

Abstract Factory

"Abstract Factory" is an object creational design pattern which separates the instantiation of groups or families of related concrete classes from the clients that use them. We can call objects instantiated by an abstract factory "products" of the factory.

This idiom is implemented by specifying an interface for the abstract factory and interfaces for all of its products; that way a client is only dependent on these interfaces and not the concrete classes that implement them.

Using the Language Translator system introduced in the last chapter, and taking a step back from dynamic class loading for the time being, we could separate the instantiation of the concrete `Translator` classes from the code that deals solely with the Translator interface.

Language Translator implementing Abstract Factory

The UML diagram in Figure 8.2 shows how both concrete classes `DefaultFactory` and `thirdparty.TransFactory` are responsible for instantiating their respective concrete `Translator` classes. The code below shows how these classes are implemented. Pay close attention to the fact that each `getLanguageInstance()` method is declared as returning a `Translator` instance, not a concrete class instance – this is the "abstract" part of Abstract Factory.

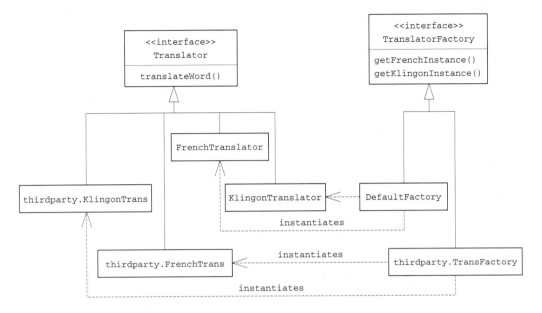

Figure 8.2 Language Translator implementing Abstract Factory

```
//Translator interface
public interface Translator
{
  public String translateWord(String word);
}

//factory interface
public interface TranslatorFactory
{
  public Translator getFrenchInstance();
  public Translator getKlingonInstance();
}

//concrete factory impls
public class DefaultFactory
  implements TranslatorFactory
{
  public Translator getFrenchInstance()
  {
    return new FrenchTranslator();
  }
  public Translator getKlingonInstance()
  {
    return new KlingonTranslator();
  }
}
```

```
//third party impl
package thirdparty;
public class TransFactory
  implements TranslatorFactory
{
  public Translator getFrenchInstance()
  {
    return new FrenchTrans ();
  }
  public Translator getKlingonInstance()
  {
    return new KlingonTrans ();
  }
}
```

Let us once again quickly take a step back and examine how we would determine which Translator to use based on a design without an abstract factory or dynamic class loading – this would involve writing code along the lines of:

```
Translator t;
if(trans_type==KLINGON)
  t= new KlingonTranslator();
else if(trans_type==THIRDPARTY_KLINGON)
  t= new thirdparty.KlingonTrans();

//etc. etc.
```

which means that the client in our example would have to know about all the concrete classes implementing the Translator interface. However, by using our new Abstract Factory implementation the client code need never be aware of the actual classes that implement the Translator interface.

```
public class Tester
{
  public static void useTranslator(TranslatorFactory tf)
  {
    Translator french=tf.getFrenchInstance();
    //method not coupled to concrete factory
    System.out.println( french );
  }
}

TranslatorFactory tf1 = new DefaultTranslator();
TranslatorFactory tf2 = new thirdparty.TransFactory();

Tester.useTranslator( tf1 );
Tester.useTranslator( tf2 );
```

Assuming that we have overridden `toString()` in the concrete `Translator` classes, the above code would produce the following output:

```
FrenchTranslator
thirdparty.FrenchTrans
```

This solves the problem of a client knowing about all the concrete classes that implement the `Translator` interface.

Using the Abstract Factory pattern adds an extra level of flexibility to a design; however, on the downside it can often lead to "fat" interfaces. Consider how "fat" our `TranslatorFactory` interface will become as we start adding all the languages we intend to support. Also, each time we add a new method to our interface all client classes would have to be recompiled and probably altered to take into account the additional interface methods. This also leads us towards another potential problem. If for example we decide to add a Norwegian translator to our system, the `Translator` `Factory` interface would have to be updated to include a `getNorwegianInstance()` method. This would force all of the other concrete factories to implement this method – nasty! One way of solving this problem would be to introduce an adapter class which provides empty implementations for additional Translators which other concrete factories can choose to support or ignore. We could implement an adapter as an abstract class as shown below, assuming we have added `getNorwegianInstance()` to `TranslatorFactory`.

Concrete classes such as `thirdparty.TransFactory` could either implement `TranslatorFactory` as before or extend `TranslatorAdapter` if they did not support one of the languages.

```
public abstract class TranslatorAdapter
  implement TranslatorFactory
{
  //methods that all translators
  //do not have to implement

  public Translator getNorwegianInstance()
    throws LanguageNotSupportedException
  {
    throw new LanguageNotSupportedException();
  }
}
```

The introduction of an adapter class solves one problem, but introduces the risk of runtime errors and diminishes the dynamics of the systems we illustrated in a previous chapter on dynamic class loading. Do not get depressed and jump forward to the next section – we are not trying to put a downer on Abstract Factory; on the contrary, as you will see later, we are just trying to make you aware of some of the pitfalls and design decisions you may encounter when using this pattern.

To solve both the problems of a fat interface and having to using conditions to determine which `Translator` our system is going to use for a particular job, we are going to modify the `TranslatorFactory` interface to allow concrete implementations to return information about the languages they support and then use that information to get the factory to return the appropriate translator. This design will allow our system to interrogate the factory and provide the end users the option of selecting which language they want to translate to, based on this information. We have opted for this design to allow each factory to use its own strategy for instantiating its Translators. For example, one implementation may use dynamic class loading, another may choose lazy instantiation or a combination of both. Keeping all of this in mind, our updated `TranslatorFactory` interface now looks like this:

```
public interface TranslatorFactory
{
  public LanguageIterator getSupportedLanguages();
  public Translator getInstance( Language lang )
     throws BadLanguageException; //illegal parameter
}
```

The method declaration `getSupportedLanguages()` requires the implementing class to return an iterator of `Language` objects. Iterators are discussed in Chapter 11.

The `Language` interface listing is as follows, where the client cannot instantiate a concrete `Language` object, but only maintain a reference to one, to be passed back to the factory to select a `Translator` object for that `Language`.

```
public interface Language
{
  public String getName();
}
```

It is an implementation detail of each concrete `TranslatorFactory` to encapsulate how it uses a `Language` object to select the appropriate Translator for that object. In our `DefaultFactory` we simply use a proxy. A proxy is an example of another idiom that we are using in this case to hide or contain the actual language translator and map that translator to a specific name.

```
class TranslatorProxy
   implements Language
{
  private String name_;
  private Translator trans_;
  //package use only
  TranslatorProxy(String name, Translator trans)
  {
    name_=name;
    trans_=trans;
  }
  public String getName() { return name_;}
  Translator getTrans() {return trans_;}
}
```

Again we have chosen to specify our `LanguageIterator` as a Java interface. This is to avoid tying third-party implementors to any specific implementation. The interface is declared as follows:

```
public interface LanguageIterator
{
  public boolean hasMoreElements();
  public Language nextElement()
    throws NoSuchElementException;
}
```

In our `DefaultFactory` we have implemented our concrete `LanguageIterator` as a wrapper around `java.util.Enumeration`, but as this concrete class is an implementation detail of `DefaultFactory`, we have made it an inner class. So why didn't we just declare `Translator.getSupportedLangauges()` as returning `java.util.Enumeration` instead of going to all the effort of implementing a wrapper around it?

There are two forces at work here, the first being type safety for collections which is investigated in a later chapter and the second being ease of use for the clients of `Translator`. By providing an explicit iterator of `Language` objects, clients do not have to go to the bother of casting each element from `Object` to `Language`. An alternative approach to using an inner class would be to declare it at package scope within the `DefaultFactory`'s package; however, as class `LangIter` is an implementation detail of `DefaultFactory` and not used by any other classes in this package we have chosen to encapsulate that detail within `DefaultFactory`. To illustrate both approaches we have placed the `TranslatorProxy` class at package scope; this class could equally have been an inner class. We reviewed some of the forces at work in this design issue in Chapter 2.

```
public class DefaultFactory
  implements TranslatorFactory
{
  private Vector translators_= new Vector();

  private class LangIter
    implements LanguageIterator
  {
    private Enumeration iter_;
    public LangIter(Enumeration e) {iter_=e;}

    public boolean hasMoreElements()
    { return iter_.hasMoreElements();}

    public Language nextElement()
      throws java.util.NoSuchElementException
    {
      return (Language)iter_.nextElement();
    }
  }
}
```

```
    public DefaultFactory()
    {
      translators_.addElement( new
        TranslatorProxy("French",new FrenchTranslator()) );
      //add other translators
    }

    //TranslatorFactory interface impl...
    public LanguageIterator getSupportedLanguages()
    {
      return new LangIter(translators_.elements());
    }
    public Translator getInstance( Language lang )
      throws BadLanguageException
    {
      if(lang instanceof TranslatorProxy)
      {
        return ((TranslatorProxy)lang).getTrans();
      }
      throw new BadLanguageException();
    }
  }
```

If you think that is a lot of information to take on board at once, we would have to agree, so to help unravel some of the key points let us take a look at how a client would use the new design. The sample code reintroduces dynamic class loading and illustrates how a client can obtain a list of supported languages from the TranslatorFactory. To keep this example simple and clear we have excluded any exception handling, and used a class with main(). In the real system we would most definitely use exceptions and our GUI would interrogate the factory and display a list of the supported languages, allowing the user the ability to select which Translator to use.

```
  public class AbFactTest
  {
    //example cmd line -- AbFactTest hello DefaultFactory

    static public void main(String [] args)
        throws Exception //dirty to simplify example
    {
      Class c=Class.forName(args[1]);
      TranslatorFactory tf=(TranslatorFactory)c.newInstance();

      LanguageIterator iter=tf.getSupportedLanguages();
      while(iter.hasMoreElements())
      {
        Language lang=iter.nextElement();
        Translator t=tf.getInstance( lang );

        String word=t.translateWord(args[0]);
```

```
     System.out.println("Langauge "+lang.getName());
     System.out.println(args[0]+" translates to "+word);
  }
 }
}
```

We would expect to invoke this application with the command line:

```
java AbFactTest hello DefaultFactory
```

Call us picky but there is still one thing that we do not like about the new design. Although we can dynamically load each TranslatorFactory, our DefaultFactory is dependent on compilation, that is, it has to know about all supported Translators to build its list of languages. Fortunately we have already seen how to postpone this decision until runtime in the last chapter.

Here is one way of reintroducing the level of flexibility illustrated in the section on dynamic class loading, without affecting any code dependent on our abstract factory. If you cast your mind back you will recall that our abstract factory was designed to allow concrete factories to choose their own strategy for implementing the getInstance() method based on the Language parameter. Our approach was to use the TranslatorProxy class to hold the name of the language and the associated Translator, and this is where the compilation dependency occurs. To resolve this design issue we have updated the TranslatorProxy class to store the language name and the implementing class name, as follows, to allow DefaultFactory to dynamically load the implementing Translator class on request. This is a form of lazy instantiation, all the gory details of which are described in the next chapter.

```
class TranslatorProxy
   implements Language
{
  private String name_;
  private String class_;

  TranslatorProxy(String name,String classname)
  {
    name_=name;
    class_=classname;
  }
  String getName() { return name_;}
  String getTransClass() {return class_;}
}
```

We now need to update our DefaultFactory so it can dynamically load the Translator class associated with the language name.

```
public class DefaultFactory
{
  //as before
```

```
public Translator getInstance( Language lang )
    throws BadLanguageException
{
  if(lang instanceof TranslatorProxy)
  {
    //exception handling omitted
    TranslatorProxy proxy=(TranslatorProxy)lang;
    Class c=Class.forName( proxy. getTransClass() );
    Translator t=(Translator)c.newInstance();
    return t;
  }
  throw new BadLanguageException();
}
}
```

To complete the new design we still have to populate the list of Language objects maintained by DefaultFactory. To do this we decided to ship an "ini" file with our system that maps the user-readable language names to their associated implementation classes, in the form

```
Language=Basic French
Impl=BasicFrench1
//etc.
```

This allows us to ship additional translators, along with a new "ini." So the final piece of the jigsaw is for DefaultFactory to read in the "ini" file and populate the list of translators.

```
private void init()
{
  String name;
  String impl_class;
  //while more entries in 'ini' file
  //get name and impl class
  //add to list of translators

  translators_.addElement( name, impl_class )
}
```

By combining an abstract factory with dynamic class loading we have been able to focus our design on usability and extensibility by allowing the client program to interrogate any translator factory that is dynamically loaded. Some other issues still remain, but are beyond the scope of this section.

You may like to consider how you could modify the design of our translator system to allow any supported language to be converted into any other supported language, rather than from English to another language. For example, a user may want to convert French directly to Klingon without first translating the word into English. This is a common problem with language translators as a word can often lose its meaning if it is translated via an intermediate language. The Visitor design pattern which uses a double-dispatch mechanism is worth investigating in this context.

Singleton

Frequently during the analysis and design process one or more classes are identified that are used to represent a system-wide resource such as a database, remote object broker, or a fixed device such as a printer. These are classes that would generally have a single shared instance, used by various other objects and subsystems. If you are working on a tiny project as the sole developer it is not too difficult to enforce the constraint that only a single instance of a class is instantiated and then passed to other objects to use. However, in any non-trivial system, with more than one developer, enforcing this constraint becomes increasingly difficult and complex if every class that uses the shared resource has to have a constructor or method that takes a copy of the shared object reference.

It is possible to make the class manage the number of instances that it can create rather than leave it as the responsibility of the developer(s). A class that can only create a single instance of itself is known as a Singleton. Often the Singleton pattern or idiom is introduced as a simple example of a pattern or idiom. We feel that this is really not the case because the Singleton is a very folded pattern – given that once you get under the covers and start to unravel it, some very interesting side effects and weird forces begin to appear. So we are going to investigate this seemingly simple pattern and examine some of these interesting effects in some depth.

In *Design Patterns* (Gamma *et al.*, 1995) the Singleton is described like this: "Ensure a class only has one instance and provide a global point of access to it." So the first question must be, how can we make sure that a class has only a single instance and make that instance easily accessible?

Let us examine the first part of that question: how can we make sure a class has only a single instance? In order for a class to instantiate a different class, that class must have a public constructor, otherwise your new friend the Java compiler will have a serious moan. We can use this knowledge to write a class that cannot be instantiated, by making the constructor private:

```
public class RemoteObjectWrapper
{
  private RemoteObjectWrapper() {}
  // ... other class details ...
}

RemoteObjectWrapper row=new RemoteObjectWrapper(); //error!!!
```

You are probably thinking that this class is totally useless as it stands, and you are right, but please bear with us. Earlier we introduced the factory method idiom, in which a method on one object or class is responsible for making another object. So why not make `RemoteObjectWrapper` a self-referencing factory? Here is how this class looks as a factory:

```
public class RemoteObjectWrapper
{
  private RemoteObjectWrapper() {}

  static public RemoteObjectWrapper getInstance()
  {
    return new RemoteObjectWrapper(); //return instance of self
  }
}
```

As the constructor is private we have made `getInstance()` a class method – static – so we can access it like this:

```
RemoteObjectWrapper.getInstance();
```

but this still leaves us with the problem that it is still possible to create multiple instances of the class. To solve this problem all we need to do is change `RemoteObject Wrapper` to contain a `static` instance variable which is a reference to an instance of an object of its own class. In formal terms this class is self-referential.

```
public class RemoteObjectWrapper
{
  private RemoteObjectWrapper() {}

  //reference to self
  static private RemoteObjectWrapper
    instance_ = new RemoteObjectWrapper();

  static public RemoteObjectWrapper getInstance()
  {
    return instance_; //the one and only instance
  }

  public void someMethod() {}
}
```

By adding the self-referencing instance variable and returning that instance we have answered both parts of the question posed earlier. We now have a class that is restricted to a single instance and is accessible to other parts of our system via its class methods – a Singleton.

```
RemoteObjectWrapper row=RemoteObjectWrapper.getInstance();
row.someMethod();
```

The generic form of the Singleton pattern in Java is listed below:

```
public class Singleton
{
  private Singleton() {}
```

```
    static private Singleton instance_
      = new Singleton();

    static public Singleton instance()
    {
      return instance_;
    }
    //public methods
  }
```

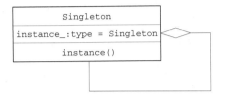

Figure 8.3 Singleton

A UML diagram showing the generic Singleton class is given in Figure 8.3.

So there you have it, your first Singleton, but there is one caveat with Singletons in Java that applies to JDK 1.1.x, namely class garbage collection.

Be aware of the potential for class garbage collection with Singletons.

JDK 1.1.x specification added the feature of class unloading, as discussed in the previous chapter. Class unloading is a powerful addition to the Java runtime as it can reduce memory usage; however, it does pose a problem when using Singletons. If clients of your Singleton always access it in the following form:

```
Singleton.instance().someMethod();
```

or by local instance variables:

```
    {
      Singleton s=Singleton.instance();
      s.someMethod();
    } //s is now out of scope - may be reclaimed by the gc
```

where the only reference to the Singleton object is maintained within the Singleton class itself, the garbage collector, in its enthusiasm to dispose of any unused trash, may assume that the Singleton is unreachable because no other object or class holds a current reference to it and could quite legally garbage collect the object and unload the class. This can cause all sorts of potential problems for Singleton classes. Consider the effect on a system that uses a Singleton class that represents a remote server. Hypothetically assume that the Singleton connects to the remote server on a call to an init() method, which is responsible for the actual connection to the remote server, based on application-specific parameters, where the other methods in the Singleton class use this connection to access the remote server. You happily write your client application making sure you invoke the init() method somewhere at the start of the program and you are up and running – or are you?

If all your client code always accesses the Singleton in either form shown above, there is a possibility that the Singleton may be garbage collected, resulting in the next method invocation forcing the Singleton to be reloaded. This could be disastrous as your program will, obviously, have been written under the assumption that the Singleton.init() method has been called. If the class has been garbage collected and subsequently reloaded, this assumption no longer holds true and fatal runtime errors result!

There are a number of ways of avoiding the garbage-collected Singleton problem. Two of the more immediate are:

- Use the -noclassgc flag when you start your program with java. For example:

  ```
  java -noclassgc mycompany.AppWithSingleton
  ```

- Maintain a registry of Singleton classes that are used by your system.

The first option may be viable if you are in control of how your system is started, but at the expense of unused classes, other than the Singletons, remaining in memory. The second option will allow your system to realize the benefits of class garbage collection, while stopping Singleton classes being trashed. The simplest way of implementing this approach is to keep a Vector of all Singleton class instances somewhere in your client code.

```
public class Client
{
  //singleton registry
  //only used to stop class gc
  private Vector singletons_
    = new Vector();

  public Client()
  {
    singletons.addElement( Singleton.instance( ) );
    //etc.
  }
}
```

This approach stops the class garbage collector because another class – Client – maintains a reference to the Singleton class instances. By the way, do not be tempted to make your Singleton registry itself a Singleton class, otherwise you will end up with the same problems that we are trying to avoid.

Singleton adapter

Earlier we also introduced the Abstract Factory design pattern. Classes implementing this pattern are frequently Singleton classes too.

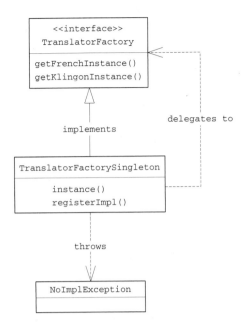

Figure 8.4 Singleton adapter

To complete our look at the Singleton we are going to examine how to create a Singleton adapter class. This idiom is useful where you have previously defined an interface and have several implementation classes available, but do not want to commit your system to a concrete Singleton implementation. As you are already familiar with our language translator system we are going to create a Singleton adapter based on the TranslatorFactory interface. The UML diagram in Figure 8.4 shows the Singleton adapter.

Source:

```
public class NoImplException extends Exception {...}

public class TranslatorFactorySingleton
  implements TranslatorFactory
{
  static private TranslatorFactorySingleton instance_;
  static private TranslatorFactory impl_; //actual impl class

  private TranslatorFactorySingleton(){}

  static public TranslatorFactorySingelton instance()
    throws NoImplException
  {
    if(impl_==null)
      throw new NoImplException();
    return instance_;
  }
```

```
static public registerImpl(TranslatorFactory impl)
{
  impl_=impl;
}


//TranslatorFactory impl
//using delegation
public LanguageIterator getSupportedLanguages()
{
  return impl_.getSupportedLanguages();
}
public Translator getInstance( Language lang )
  throws BadLanguageException
{
  return impl_.getInstance(lang);
}
}
```

Given the Singleton adapter class we can update our earlier example where the concrete TranslatorFactory is dynamically loaded as follows, thus making that implementation available to our system through a Singleton:

```
static public void main(String [] args)
{
  Class c= Class.forName(args[1]);
  TranslatorFactory ft= (TranslatorFactory)c.newInstance();
  //register as the current implementation.
  TranslatorFactorySingleton.registerImpl( ft );

  TranslatorFactorySingleton inst
    = TranslatorFactorySingleton.instance();

  //remember to keep a reference to the actual singleton
  //to avoid class gc in JDK 1.1.x
  singletons_.addElement( inst );
}
```

Apart from the extra registerImpl() class method which is necessary at "start up" time, TranslatorFactorySingleton acts just like a normal Singleton.

We hope that you now have a clearer view of the Singleton and some extensions to the basic Singleton that are possible in Java. The Singleton is a fascinating pattern – and idiom – in Java.

To wind up this chapter we are going to take a look at an alternative approach to using factory methods, by moving the responsibility into a concrete class's constructor.

"Virtual" Constructor idiom

Earlier we mentioned that it is possible to have a factory method (*Virtual Constructor*) that actually looks like a constructor. The motivation behind this approach is to make it transparent to the client as to which implementation class is actually doing the work.

If you cast your mind back to an example we used before, evolving an employee system which modeled various types of company employees and pay models, all concrete employee classes had to implement the Employee interface, so in order to instantiate a employee object we used the following form:

```
Employee e= new FatCatEmployee(...);
Employee e2= new LowPaidEmployee(...);
```

By *virtualizing* the constructor we can make the client code appear as follows:

```
Employee e= new CompanyEmployee(/* param */);
```

To understand how this works in practice let us examine how CompanyEmployee implements its constructor. To keep the example simple we have used condition statements in the constructor to determine which type of concrete Employee to instantiate. Any number of different approaches could be taken to determine the concrete type, but again for simplicity we are simply passing a typesafe constant as a parameter.

```
public class CompanyEmployee
  implements Employee
{
  private Employee employee_; //holds ref. to concrete class

  public CompanyEmployee(EmpType type /* other params*/)
  {
    if(type==EmpType.FAT_CAT)
      employee_= new FatCatEmployee(/*params*/);
    if(type==EmpType.LOW_PAID)
      employee_= new LowPaidEmployee(/*params*/);
    //see abstract factory and double dispatch for
    //alternative approaches to if/else
  }

  //Employee methods delegate to employee_
  public float calcAnnualBonus(PayModel pm)
  {
    return employee_.calcAnnualBonus( pm );
  }
}

//client code
Employee e= new CompanyEmployee(EmpType.FAT_CAT);
Employee e2= new CompanyEmployee(EmpType.LOW_PAID);
```

The above implementation of this idiom offers the advantage of potentially less complex client code at the expense of a greater maintenance effort as CompanyEmployee has to know about all possible concrete implementations of the Employee interface. However, we can improve the design by encapsulating the use of a Singleton Abstract Factory within the constructor of CompanyEmployee as follows:

```
//constructor
public CompanyEmployee(EmpType type /* other params*/)
{
  EmployeeFactory empFactory=EmpFactory.getInstance();
  employee_=empFactory.make( type );
}
```

By combining the three idioms Singleton, Abstract Factory, and Virtual Constructor we can simplify the client code and still design a dynamic and loosely coupled system.

We have only had time to start to scratch at the surface of the many different implementations and forms the idioms presented can take. The last example illustrates one of many possible combinations of these idioms. For example, we could have declared the Language interface, introduced earlier, as an abstract factory allowing clients to invoke a makeTranslator() method directly, or used the EmployeeFactory above directly, instead of encapsulating its usage with a constructor. We hope that you will leave this chapter inspired to find your own ways of implementing the idioms that solve design problems specific to your domain.

SUMMARY

The field of creational patterns is based largely around the notion of an object factory. By using factories in various ways we can make other patterns such as Abstract Factories and Singletons, along with a host of variations on this theme.

We can use Abstract Factories to create frameworks around which we can evolve and generate new concrete classes and use them within this "plug and play" architecture. The combination of Abstract Factories and dynamic class loading by name allows us to build incredibly flexible systems that encourage organic rather than monolithic system development. This is particularly suitable to Web-based and distributed systems design.

Singletons are very useful for objects that represent singular entities in a system. When using Singletons be aware of the potential for class garbage collection – this may or may not be implemented in the JVM you are using.

9 Balancing performance and resource usage

Lazy instantiation

Eager instantiation

Lazy evaluation

Eager evaluation

Introduction

The balance between the performance of software and the resources that it consumes has been an issue since the "birth" of computers and stems from the need to conserve valuable resources such as memory, possibly at the expense of performance. While we are writing this book 64 MB of on-board RAM in a personal computer is considered the standard requirement, but by the time you read this it may have doubled! It was not so long ago (in geological terms) that we were thrilled at the prospect of the on-board memory in an eight-bit microcomputer jumping from 8 K to 64 K. In those days the only sensible option was to write at a machine code level for non-trivial programs.

Judging by the ever increasing resource hungry applications we use now, it is amazing that anybody ever managed to write a program to fit into that tiny amount of memory. Even though we have much more memory to play with these days, there are some valuable lessons to learn from the techniques established to work within such tight constraints.

Java programming is not just about writing applets and applications for deployment on personal computers and workstations – Java has made strong inroads into the embedded systems market. Current embedded systems have relatively scarce resources and computing power so many of the old issues have resurfaced for Java developers working in this field. Balancing these factors is a fascinating design problem as we have to understand that no solution in this area of design is going to be perfect. So what we need to do is understand the types of techniques that are going to be useful in achieving the fine balance required to work within the constraints of the deployment platform.

Let us start by taking an example. If you are familiar with Netscape's Web browser and have used both versions 3.x and 4.x you will have undoubtedly noticed a difference in how the Java runtime is loaded. If you look at the splash screen when Netscape 3 starts up you will see it loading various resources, including Java. However, when you start up

Netscape 4.x it does not load the Java runtime, but waits until you visit a Web page that includes the <APPLET> tag. These two different approaches illustrate the techniques of "eager instantiation" (load it just in case it is needed) and "lazy instantiation" (wait until it is requested, as it may never be needed).

There are benefits to both approaches. On the one hand, always loading a resource is wasteful in terms of memory usage if it is not used during that session and on the other hand, if it has not been loaded you pay the price for loading when the resource is first required. Some people may also use the terms optimistic and pessimistic to describes these strategies. Either way this trade-off is so common in software design that it is worth spending some time to understand the pros and cons of each strategy.

Lazy instantiation

Lazy instantiation in Java falls into two categories:

- Lazy class loading
- Lazy object creation.

The Java runtime has built-in lazy instantiation for classes. Classes are only loaded into memory when they are first referenced. Here is a quick reminder of when classes get loaded into memory. They may also be loaded from a Web server via http first.

```
MyUtils.classMethod();    //first call to a static class method
Vector v = new Vector(); //first call to operator new
```

Lazy class loading is an important feature of the Java runtime environment as it can reduce memory usage under certain circumstances. For example, if a part of a program is never executed during a session, classes that are only referenced in that part of the program will never be loaded.

Lazy instantiation of objects

Lazy object creation is tightly coupled to lazy class loading, as shown above. The first time you use the new keyword on a class type that has not previously been loaded the Java runtime will take care of loading it for you. Lazy object creation can be used to reduce memory usage to a much greater extent than lazy class loading. To introduce the concept of lazy object creation, let us take a look at a simple code example where a Frame uses a MessageBox to display error messages.

```
public class MyFrame extends Frame
{
  private MessageBox mb_ = new MessageBox();

  //private helper used by this class
  private void showMessage(String message)
```

```
  {
    //set the message text
    mb_.setMessage( message );
    mb_.pack();
    mb_.show();
  }
}
```

In the above example, when an instance of MyFrame is created the MessageBox instance mb_ is also created. The same rules apply recursively. So any instance variables initialized or assigned in class MessageBox's constructor are also allocated off the heap and so on. If the instance of MyFrame does not display an error message within a session we are wasting memory unnecessarily. In this rather simple example we are not really going to gain too much, but if you consider a more complex class which uses many other classes, which in turn use and instantiate more objects recursively, the potential memory usage is more apparent.

Ⓣ Consider lazy instantiation as a policy to reduce resource requirements.

The lazy approach to the above example is listed below, where the object mb_ is instantiated on the first call to showMessage(); that is, not until it is actually needed by the program.

```
public final class MyFrame extends Frame
{
  private MessageBox mb_ ; //null, implicit

  //private helper used by this class
  private void showMessage(String message)
  {
    if(mb_==null) //first call to this method
      mb_=new MessageBox();

    //set the message text
    mb_.setMessage( message );
    mb_.pack();
    mb_.show();
  }
}
```

If you take a closer look at showMessage() you will see that we first check if the instance variable mb_ is equal to null. As we have not initialized mb_ at its point of declaration, the Java runtime has taken care of this for us, thus we can safely proceed by creating the MessageBox instance. All future calls to showMessage() will find that mb_ is not equal to null, therefore skipping the creation of the object and using the existing instance.

Let us now examine a more realistic example where lazy instantiation can play a key role in reducing the amount of resources used by a program.

Assume we have been asked by a client to write a system that will let users catalog images on a file system and provide the facility to view either thumbnails or complete images. Our first attempt might be to write a class which loads the image in its constructor:

```
public class ImageFile
{
  private String filename_;
  private Image image_;

  public ImageFile(String filename)
  {
    filename_=filename;
    //load the image
  }
  public String getName(){ return filename_;}
  public Image getImage()
  {
    return image_;
  }
}
```

In the example above, ImageFile is implementing an "over eager" approach to instantiating the Image object. Not only could this be painfully slow, in the case of a directory containing many images, but this design could exhaust the available memory. In its favor, this design guarantees that an image will be available immediately at the time of a call to getImage(). To avoid these potential problems we can trade the performance benefits of instantaneous access for reduced memory usage. As you may have guessed, we can achieve this by using lazy instantiation. Here is the updated ImageFile class using the same approach as class MyFrame did with its MessageBox instance variable:

```
public class ImageFile
{
  private String filename_;
  private Image image_; //=null, implicit

  public ImageFile(String filename)
  {
    //only store the filename
    filename_=filename;
  }
  public String getName(){ return filename_;}
  public Image getImage()
  {
    if(image_==null)
```

```
    {
        //first call to getImage()
        //load the image ...
    }
    return image_;
  }
}
```

In our latest incarnation, the actual image is only loaded on the first call to getImage(). So to recap, the trade-off here is that to reduce the overall memory usage and start-up times, we pay the price for loading the image the first time it is requested, introducing a performance hit at that point in the program's execution. This is another idiom which reflects the Proxy pattern in a context that requires a constrained use of memory.

The policy of lazy instantiation illustrated above is fine for our examples, but later on you will see how the design has to alter in the context of multiple threads.

In Chapter 8 we introduced the Singleton pattern and gave the generic listing of the pattern in Java. In the generic version we declared and initialized the instance_ field as follows:

```
static final Singleton instance_ = new Singleton();
```

Readers familiar with the GOF implementation of Singleton (which is given in C++) may have been surprised that we did not defer the initialization of the instance_ field until the call to the instance() method, thus using lazy instantiation:

```
public Singleton instance()
{
    if(instance_==null) //Lazy instantiation
        instance_= new Singleton();

    return instance_;
}
```

The listing above is a direct port of the C++ Singleton example given by the GOF and is frequently touted as the generic Java version too. If you are already familiar with this form and were surprised that we did not list our generic Singleton like this, you will be even more surprised to learn that it is totally unnecessary in Java! This is a common example of what can occur if you port code from one language to another without considering the respective runtime environments.

For the record, the GOF's C++ version of Singleton uses lazy instantiation because there is no guarantee of the order of static initialization of objects at runtime (see Scott Meyers' (1995) Singleton for an alternative approach in C++). In Java we do not have to worry about these issues.

P Avoid lazy instantiation for concrete Singleton classes.

The main reason why the lazy approach to instantiating a Singleton in Java is unnecessary is due to the way in which the Java runtime handles class loading and static instance variable initialization. Previously we have described how and when classes get loaded. A class with only public static methods gets loaded by the Java runtime on the first call to one of these methods, which in the case of our Singleton is:

```
Singleton s=Singleton.instance();
```

The first call to `Singleton.instance()` in a program forces the Java runtime to load the class Singleton. As the field `instance_` is declared as `static`, the Java runtime will initialize it after successfully loading the class, thus guaranteeing that the call to `Singleton.instance()` will return a fully initialized Singleton – get the picture?

Make methods using lazy instantiation "thread safe," if they can be called either directly or indirectly by client classes.

Using lazy instantiation for a concrete Singleton is not only unnecessary in Java, it is downright dangerous in the context of multi-threaded applications. Consider the lazy version of the `Singleton.instance()` method where two or more separate threads are attempting to obtain a reference to the object via `instance()`. If one thread is pre-empted after successfully executing the line `if(instance_==null)`, but before it has completed the line `instance_=new Singleton()`, another thread can also enter this method with `instance_` still `==null` – nasty! The outcome of this scenario is the likelihood that one or more Singleton objects will be created. This is a major headache when your Singleton class is, say, connecting to a database or remote server. The simple solution to this problem would be to use the `synchronized` keyword to protect the method from multiple threads entering it at the same time:

```
synchronized static public instance() {...}
```

However, this approach is a bit heavy handed for most multi-threaded applications that are using a Singleton class extensively, causing blocking on concurrent calls to `instance()`. By the way, invoking a synchronized method is always much slower than invoking a non-synchronized one. So what we need is a strategy for synchronization that does not cause unnecessary blocking. Fortunately such a strategy exists and is known as the *double-check* idiom.

Use the double-check idiom to protect methods using lazy instantiation.

Here is how to implement it in Java:

```
public Singleton instance()
{
    if(instance_==null) //don't want to block here
    {
        //two or more threads might be here!!!

        synchronized(Singleton.class)
        {
            //must check again as one of the
            //blocked threads can still enter
```

```
    if(instance_==null)
        instance_= new Singleton(); //safe
    }
  }
  return instance_;
}
```

The double-check idiom improves performance by only using synchronization if multiple threads call instance() before the Singleton is constructed. Once the object has been created and any waiting threads have entered/exited the synchronized block, this block will not be used again during the remaining lifetime of the Singleton.

Using multiple threads in Java can be very complex; in fact the topic of concurrency is so vast that Doug Lea (1997) has written a whole book on the subject, *Concurrent Programming in Java*. We would recommend that you get your hands on a copy of this book if you are new to concurrent programming, before you embark on writing complex Java systems that rely on multiple threads.

Eager instantiation

Eager instantiation is the direct opposite of lazy instantiation. As with its counterpart, eager instantiation falls into the same categories for the Java language, namely class loading and object creation.

To perform eager instantiation of classes you can use the Class.forName() method without paying the price for instantiating an object. The example below shows a method that takes an array of String objects and forces the classes to be loaded.

```
public Class [] loadClasses(String [] classnames)
  throws ClassNotFoundException
{
  int num = classnames.length;
  Class [] classes= new Class[ num ];
  for(int i=0; i< num; i++)
  {
    classes[i]=Class.forName( classnames[i] );
  }
  return classes;
}
```

The method loadClasses() returns an array of Class objects for the client to use. There is a potential problem lurking underneath the surface here for some JDK 1.1 implementations, namely class garbage collection; however, this technique simply illustrates that you can be as eager with your approach to class loading as you can be to down that first beer on a Friday night!

One example where eager class loading can be effective is to show a percentage loaded progress bar while an applet or application is starting up. As object instantiation and class loading are interdependent, a better approach to eager instantiation might be to preload objects that you know you are going to need to be available to your program early in its execution cycle, thus increasing its liveliness.

To illustrate this, we are going to examine the client end of a system which connects to a remote server. The users of the client software have to enter a user name and password to access the system. Two sequential approaches that could be used when the client program starts are listed below.

- Start

    Connect to remote server
    Show login prompt
    Verify user

- Start

    Show login prompt
    Connect to server
    Verify user

There is a trade-off between the two approaches. In the first approach the program connects to the remote server before showing the login prompt, trading a longer visible wait for the user of the system for the ability to report that the server is down/unavailable if the connection fails. Whereas the second approach trades the ability to provide a faster start-up, from the user's perspective, for the potential horror of the server not being available after attempting to connect. Also keep in mind that for each of the steps in both approaches, classes and objects will need to be loaded/created as they are encountered within the program's execution path.

Another approach entirely would be to use a separate thread of execution to perform one of the tasks, such as connecting to the remote server – this is how we can implement an eager instantiation policy. The sample code below shows this in action. We have defined the interface CompletionCallback to allow an object to be notified when the EagerConnection thread instance has completed or failed.

RemoteServerProxy is a Singleton class which handles connections to the real remote server. The class EagerConnection simply attempts to connect to the remote server in the run() method, which is executed when start() is called on a Thread.

```
public interface CompletionCallback
{
  public void operationComplete(Object src);
  public void operationFailed(Exception ex);
}
//Exception
public class RemoteServerEx extends Exception {...}

//Singleton
public class RemoteServerProxy
{
  static private RemoteServerProxy instance_
    = new RemoteServerProxy();
```

```
    private RemoteServerProxy() {}

    static public RemoteServerProxy instance()
    { return instance_;}

    public void connect(/* parameters */)
       throws RemoteServerEx //defined elsewhere
    {...}
    public void verifyUser(/*parameters */)
       throws RemoteServerEx
    {...}
}

public class EagerConnection
   implements Runnable
{
   private CompletionCallback compcb_;

   public EagerConnection( CompletionCallback cc)
   { compcb_=cc; }

   public void run()
   {
      try
      {
      //forces class and dependants to load
      //creates object and dependants
      RemoteServerProxy rs=RemoteServerProxy.instance();
      rs.connect();
      compcb_.operationComplete(this);
      }
      //see Chapter 5 for delegated exception handling
      catch(InteruptedException ex)
      {
         compcb_.operationFailed(ex);
      }
      catch(RemoteServerEx ex)
      {
         compcb_.operationFailed(ex);
      }
    }
  }
```

The class EagerConnection simply connects to the remote server by using the RemoteServerProxy Singleton. On completion or if an exception is encountered, the run() method uses the CompletionCallback to notify the caller.

Below is the client code that uses the RemoteServerProxy and EagerConnection classes. For this example we have chosen to use a completion callback to notify the program that a valid connection has been established or that an exception occurred

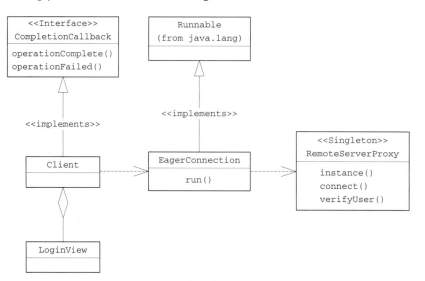

Figure 9.1 Eager connection class diagram

(for delegated exception handling see Chapter 5; for callback see Chapter 6). An alternative approach to using a completion callback in this case would be to use `join()` on the thread instance `eagerConnectionThread` and employ a different mechanism to indicate failures.

The UML class diagram is shown in Figure 9.1.

```java
public class Client
   implements CompletionCallback
{
   static public void main(String [] args)
   {
      Client client= new Client();

      //start background connection thread
      //which loads related classes and creates
      //object required to communicate with
      //the remote server

      EagerConnection connect = new EagerConnection( client );
      Thread eagerConnectionThread = new Thread( connect );
      eagerConnectionThread.start();

      //now carry on and show login prompt while
      //EagerConnection tries to connect to the remote server
   }

   //CompletionCallback impl
   public void operationComplete(Object src)
   { /* Everything OK */}
```

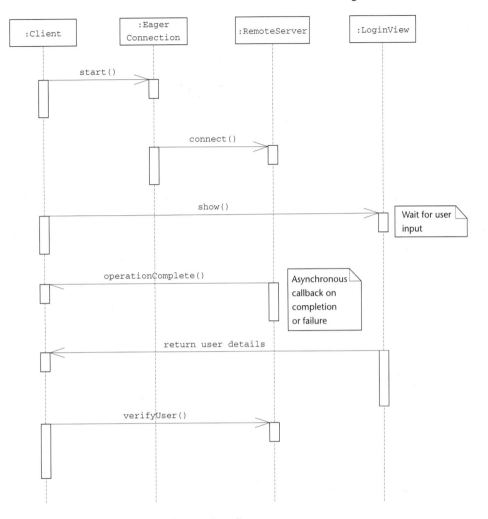

Figure 9.2 Eager connection interaction diagram

```
public void operationFailed(Exception ex)
{
   //delegated exception handler for thread
   //take action
}
}
```

The UML interaction diagram in Figure 9.2 shows one possible interaction. In this scenario RemoteServerProxy completes its connection before the user has entered his or her details. As the call to RemoteServerProxy.connect() is asynchronous it could equally well return after or at the same time as the user details are returned from the LoginView. The important thing to grasp here is that by using a separate thread to perform the remote server connections, we are implicitly loading classes and creating objects ready to be used at a later time – eager instantiation.

Having examined both the eager and lazy instantiation of classes and objects, we are now going to investigate how we can use similar policies, but relating to expressions and calculations – generally known as lazy and eager evaluations. As with instantiation, each evaluation policy has its pros and cons. In the next section we hope to be able to enlighten you as we investigate further.

Lazy evaluation

Hopefully if you have been following the plot you might already be thinking about how you can be lazy in other areas of your Java code too. Although the terms lazy and eager evaluation have their roots in parameter passing for functional programming languages, we can apply some of the principles in Java. For lazy evaluation they fall into two main categories:

- Expression evaluations
- Calculations.

As everyone who has studied for their Java programmer exam knows, the order in which expressions are evaluated is important. By changing the way we write expressions in Java we can use this knowledge to improve the performance of our programs.

Possibly the simplest way to start is by reviewing the boolean/conditional OR operator. The Java language specification states that operands in a conditional OR are evaluated from left to right and if the first operand is true, the second operand is not checked.

Given that the following expression

```
if( true || false )
```

is always going to yield true, we can start to use this to our advantage. Take a close look at the expression below:

```
if ( (x/100)<20 || y<10 )
```

Simply by reversing the operands we can immediately save on the cost of the division $x/100$ if y is less than 10.

```
if( y<10 || (x/100)<20 )
```

You might be thinking, "Hang on for a second, surely this is an optimization trick." We should only optimize code when the need arises. OK, this is a kind of optimization, but one that is in effect free. It does not obfuscate code or require that we change anything other than the order in which we construct these expressions. It is certainly worth taking a couple of minutes to think about as you code up these expressions because lazy expression evaluation gets more interesting and effective when you start to introduce more time-consuming elements such as method calls.

As an example we have made a small e-mail application. In this example we are using two method calls. The first method call returns a boolean that determines if the users are interested in reading their messages at the moment. The second call is to ask the mailbag, which is a container, to count the number of messages that have arrived and that are ready to read. So if there are no items to be read or the user does not want to read the mail we do not need to do anything.

```
boolean read_messages = readMessages();
int num_items=mailbag.countItems();

if(num_items>0 &&  read_messages) {...}
```

The example above uses the boolean/condition AND operator &&, and as you know operands are evaluated from left to right. When an operand evaluates to false the remaining operands are not checked because the whole expression cannot be true. Keeping that in mind, we can immediately improve the code by reversing the operands and moving a method call into the conditional statement:

```
boolean read_messages=readMessages();
int num_items;

if(read_messages && (num_items=mailbag.countItems())>0)
{
  //use num_items
}
```

Notice that we have also moved the assignment of the variable num_items into the condition statement. We agree that this kind of code is ugly and we will come back to that, but for the moment it has served a valid purpose – to avoid the overhead of an additional call to countItems() if the conditional statement yields false.

So what have we actually gained by reordering the operand? We mentioned earlier that an && conditional statement "drops out" as soon as it encounters an expression that evaluates to false. In our example, that means if read_messages==false we do not pay the price of invoking mailbag.countItems().

An alternative, less hideous, approach would be to separate the conditions in the if statement as follows, achieving the desired effect. We have also introduced the use of an iterator (see Chapter 11) to avoid the overhead of forcing the mailbag to count the number of items it contains as we are not going to use the num_items variable in this code example.

```
if(readMessages())
{
  Iterator iter=mailbag.getIterator();
  for( iter.first();!iter.isDone();iter.next() )
  {
    Object o=iter.currentItem();
    //process items
  }
}
```

Once you become familiar with lazy evaluations you will forget that they seem like optimization tricks and just treat them as useful programming skills.

Let us now take a look at the other form of lazy evaluation, namely calculations. By calculations we do not mean primitive-type calculations such as x/100, but calculations such as counting the number of items in a container after it has been split or merged. These are class-specific operations which can affect memory usage and performance. To illustrate the technique of lazy calculation we are going to use the example of a charting component that can display any number of overlaid data sets. The part of the chart component we are interested in is a method which calculates the maximum, minimum, and average values of the data sets and displays the results as three overlaid charts. To get a feel for how the component works, here is a cut-down version including brief explanations.

```
public class Chart extends Panel
{
  public void addDataSet(double [] data, String label)
  {
    //add a data set with an unique label
  }
  public void showMaxMinAvg()
  {
    //calculate the max/min/avg values, then display
  }
  //other methods
}
```

There are two potential strategies that could be used to perform the calculation in showMaxMinAvg(), either eager or lazy. Using the eager approach we would calculate the results each time a new data set is added to the component and cache the results, ready to be used when showMaxMinAvg() is invoked, but we are going to be lazy and calculate the results only when they are required. The trade-off here is whether to pay the price in terms of performance when data is added to the component and in memory usage by caching the results (eager approach), or pay the price when showMaxMinAvg() is invoked (lazy). The answers to these questions will be determined by factors such as the particular system you are writing, the runtime environment, and the end user's expectations/requirements. Frequently there is a compromise between the two strategies, allowing you to be both lazy and eager. In this example the compromise is at the cost of some additional memory usage.

```
public class Chart extends Panel
{
  private double [][] maxminavg_;
  private boolean dirty_=true;

  public void addDataSet(double [] data, String label)
  {
    dirty_=true; //flag that a new data set has arrived
    //add a data set with an unique label
  }
```

```
public void showMaxMinAvg()
{
  if(dirty_)
{
  //calculate the max/min/avg values
  //Store results in cache
}
  //display the cached results
  }
//other methods
}
```

To achieve the compromise of both eager and lazy evaluation in our chart example we have introduced a cache to store the calculation results in and a `dirty_` flag to indicate when a new data set is added (or removed), thus invalidating the cache. `showMaxMinAvg()` simply checks the `dirty_` flag and either recalculates or uses the existing results.

Before leaving lazy evaluation, it is worth back-tracking a little to the earlier example that used a collection instance `mailbag`. In that example we mentioned that `mailbag.countItems()` counted its number of items on request, thus implementing lazy evaluation. We used this example to illustrate that in some cases, such as where a collection is actually an abstraction over objects in a multi-user database, lazy evaluation may be the only viable approach to returning the current number of items in that collection. The actual implementation details of a collection class should not normally be of concern to the client classes because they are encapsulated; however, it is often worth checking the documentation that accompanies class libraries to see what it says about individual class behavior.

Eager evaluation

In the previous section we touched briefly on an eager evaluation policy that we could have employed in our `Chart` example, but we opted for using a lazy policy. In this section we are going to look at a different example; in this case it makes more sense to do as much of the computation as early as we possibly can.

In this example we have been working on a lightweight Button class, the like of which you might find in the Swing component set.

In order for layout managers to work with a component in the AWT it is the responsibility of the component to implement three methods that the layout manager can call on, to establish the minimum size, the preferred size, and the maximum size that this component may be. In these methods you may often see code of the following form:

```
class LightButton extends Canvas
{
  private final int MIN_X = 10;
  private final int MIN_Y = 10;
```

```
// ...

public Dimension getMinimumSize()
{
  return new Dimension(MIN_X, MIN_Y);
}
// ...
}
```

Using a profiler we have seen that every time the layout containing the button calls the getMinimumSize() method on the LightButton, we are creating a new Dimension object. This is wasting processor time and creating a lot of garbage. This is simply unnecessary as we have previously decided that the minimum size for the LightButton is going to be fixed, hence the use of final ints to store the minimum x and y sizes. Keeping that in mind, we can simply create an instance of the Dimension at the time we construct the LightButton object and continually return that object whenever the layout manager calls the getMinimumSize() method.

```
class LightButton extends Canvas
{
  private final int MIN_X = 10;
  private final int MIN_Y = 10;
  private final Dimension minDimension_
    = new Dimension(MIN_X, MIN_Y); //Eager evaluation
  // ...

  public Dimension getMinimumSize()
  {
    return minDimension_;
  }
  // ...
}
```

Now we have stopped a new Dimension object being created for each call to the method, but we can be even more "eager" than this. We know that the minimum size of the button will not vary from button instance to button instance so we can move the Dimension-related objects to static class-based information. This means that we create the minDimension_ of the button at class load time and share it among all of the instances of LightButton. This makes our button even "lighter" because we do not carry the instance objects in each instance, making all of the instances of the button consume less memory and construct faster.

```
class LightButton extends Canvas
{
  private static final int MIN_X = 10;
  private static final int MIN_Y = 10;
  private static final Dimension minDimension_
    = new Dimension(MIN_X, MIN_Y);
  // ...
```

```java
public Dimension getMinimumSize()
{
  return minDimension_;
}
// ...
}
```

In this case it makes sense to create these objects as early as possible and share these static objects out among all instances in the LightButton, as it gives us both a performance and a memory advantage. However, we can only do this because we have decided at design time that this information is not going to vary.

SUMMARY

Eager and lazy strategies for both instantiation and evaluation exert different forces during the design and implementation of a software system. Frequently trade-offs have to be made to satisfy users' expectations or to utilize scarce resources efficiently. Understanding the techniques for implementing lazy and eager strategies coupled with the rich set of features that the Java language and runtime environment offer can help you design elegant, efficient, and fast software systems.

10 Collections

Introduction

Collection classes are used to group together object instances in a manageable way. Generally they provide a set of methods to access and manipulate the objects they contain, such as add, get, and delete. Instances of collection classes are often referred to as containers.

Under the hood, various mainly dynamic data structures may be used to implement the methods defined in a collection's interface; examples of these are linked lists, hash tables, and binary trees. Good designs avoid dependencies between the implementation details of collection classes and the classes that use or manipulate their data. The aim of this chapter is to describe various techniques and idioms that can help you design more robust and flexible systems using collections.

A standard collection class

We are going to start by taking a look at one of Java's standard collection classes, java.lang.Vector, and examine its usage. Vector represents an expandable array of objects known as elements and is a heterogeneous collection class. This means that any instance of, or subclass of, the class Object can be added to it. We could add a String followed by a URL (Uniform Resource Locator) instance in an attempt to create a list of our favorite Web sites, according to the rule that every Web site's readable name is followed by the URL of the site.

```
Vector v = new Vector();
v.addElement("Javasoft's home page");
v.addElement( new URL("http://www.javasoft.com" ) );
```

Vectors may be described as heterogeneous in that they are totally flexible with respect to the type of classes which they contain. However, this extreme flexibility can result in a considerable programming effort to ensure that the correct element types and their order within the collection are known and used accordingly. So to retrieve and use the elements in the Vector above we would have to write code like that shown below. (An alternative approach would be to use an Enumeration, but we are saving that for the next chapter.)

```
int size=v.size();
for(int i=0;i<size;i+=2)
{
   String description=(String)v.elementAt(i);
   URL url=(URL)v.elementAt(i+1);
   System.out.println(""+description+" "+url);
}
```

A sole developer working on a project may be able to use this approach successfully. With a shared Vector, however, the chances are that when more than one developer is involved someone else might add the objects to the Vector in the wrong order, ultimately leading to a ClassCastException when the elements are retrieved in the excepted order, or they may forget to add one of the elements to the Vector, resulting in an ArrayIndexOutOfBoundsException on a call to elementAt().

Some pundits argue that heterogeneous collections are bad news as they are prone to runtime exceptions, as we have illustrated above; however, our experience has shown that, if used correctly, heterogeneous collections such as Vector can be used effectively without the risk of runtime errors. We agree that, if used as above, heterogeneous collections can be a problem, but in well-designed and encapsulated classes they pose no threat to the Java runtime. A big benefit of heterogeneous collections is that they reduce the overall size of a system; however, as you will see later on this chapter, there are cases where homogenous (more specific) collections can be more effective.

A simple solution to one of the problems illustrated above would be to define a class that contains both a String and a URL object and use it instead of adding a String followed by a URL. This removes the risk of elements being added in the wrong order or being omitted from the collection.

```
public class FavoriteURL
{
   private String description_;
   private URL url_;
   public FavoriteURL( String description,URL url )
   {
      description_=description;
      url_=url;
   }
   public final String getDescription() { return description_;}
   public final URL getURL() {return url_;}
}

FavoriteURL fav=
new FavoriteURL("JavaSoft ",new URL("http://www.javasoft.com"));
Vector v= new Vector();
v.addElement( fav );
```

By encapsulating the `String` and `URL` objects into the class `FavoriteURL` we can avoid the problem of `URL` and `String` objects being added in the wrong order. However, this will not help us if another developer decides, for whatever reason, to add a `Spanner` object to the `Vector`. You may think actions such as this are unlikely and in a well-designed system they should be, but it is worth keeping this in mind as we take a look at collections that are more specific to the objects that they contain.

Homogenous collections

Homogenous collection classes are those that only permit the adding and retrieval of objects of a known type. There are several approaches to writing homogenous collections, each with their own strengths and weaknesses. In our first example we are going to define a typesafe homogenous collection of `FavoriteURL` objects.

Typesafe collections

```
public class FavoriteURLVector
{
  private Vector elements_= new Vector();

  public void addElement(FavoriteURL furl)
  {
    elements_.addElement( furl );
  }
  public FavoriteURL elementAt( int index )
  {
    return (FavoriteURL)elements_.elementAt( index );
  }
}
```

Given the above class, the compiler will enforce that only instances of `FavoriteURL` can be added to the collection.

```
FavoriteURLVector fcv= new FavoriteURLVector();
FavoriteURL fav=
new FavoriteURL("UK Soccer league",
new URL("http://www.fa-carling.com") );
fcv.addElement( fav );              //okay
fcv.addElement( new Spanner() ); //compiler error
```

Another benefit of our new `FavoriteURLVector` is that client code can be written directly in terms of `FavoriteURL` without the need to cast from `Object`. The main benefit here is readability and clarity of the client code.

```
FavoriteURL fav=fcv.elementAt(0); //no cast required
```

You may be wondering why we did not declare `FavoriteURLVector` as extending `java.util.Vector`.

There are two reasons:

- `Vector.elementAt()` is declared `final` so we cannot override it – even if it was not declared final you cannot override a method with the same parameters, but with a different return type.

- If we had extended `Vector` and provided a `getFavoriteURL()` method to get around item 1, our collection would still contain an `addElement(Object element)` method, allowing `Spanner` and other objects to be added, thus making our collection heterogeneous, not homogenous.

A good, or bad, example, depending on your perspective, of extending `java.util.Vector` comes in the form of `java.util.Stack`. A stack represents a last-in-first-out (LIFO) list of objects, with the constraint that objects can only be added (pushed) or removed (popped) from the top of the stack. So we have a problem: by extending `Vector`, `Stack` cannot enforce these constraints. The example below shows this in action by pushing three objects onto a stack and then using the inherited method `elementAt()` to retrieve an object in the middle of the stack, thus breaking the constraints normally associated with a stack.

```java
import java.util.*;

public class Main
{
  public static void main(String [] args)
  {
    Stack stack= new Stack();
    stack.push("Object 1");
    stack.push("Object 2");
    stack.push("Object 3");
    //Stack constraints broken on next line
    Object obj2=stack.elementAt(1); //inherited from Vector
    System.out.println( obj2 );
  }
}
```

For these reasons we prefer the use of delegation. However, there is a downside to using delegation, in that we have to duplicate all the methods of the implementation class that we want to make `public`. So in the case of our `FavoriteURLVector` we may want to also support the methods `isEmpty()` and `size()`, forcing us to write the delegation methods as follows:

```java
public class FavoriteURLVector
{
  //as before

  public boolean isEmpty()
  { return elements_.isEmpty();}
```

```
    public int size()
    { return elements_.size();}
}
```

To summarize our first look at homogenous collection classes we can state that we have gained type safety at the expense of the introduction of an additional class (FavoriteURLVector). If we were to make every suitable collection class homogenous in a system we could well end up with a proliferation of additional classes adding to the overall size of the system. The best candidates for homogenous collection classes are those that are intended for reuse outside the current context. For example, a StringVector class that only allows the adding and removal of String objects is a prime candidate for reuse. Just think how many times you have used or are likely to use a Vector of String objects!

Using delegation again, we can easily write a reusable StringVector class that has the benefits listed above.

```
package collections;

public class StringVector
{
  private Vector elements_= new Vector();

  public void addElement(String str)
  {
    elements_.addElement( str );
  }
  public String elementAt( int index )
  {
    return (String)elements_.elementAt( index );
  }
}
```

Once again we would have to use delegation to implement isEmpty(), size(), and so on in StringVector – or do we?

Assume that you have been asked to develop a package of typesafe collections such as StringVector, IntegerVector, DateVector, and so on. How would you go about implementing the delegated methods that each collection class requires – by using cut and paste? Hopefully not, because what we have just described is behavior that is common to all of the proposed collection classes. This sounds like a job for generalization – the process of migrating common behavior and instance variables to a superclass.

```
package collections;

class CollectionImpl
{
  private Vector elements_ = new Vector();
  public final boolean isEmpty()
  { return elements_.isEmpty();}
```

```
public final int size()
{ return elements_.size();}

protected final Object get(int index)
{ return elements_.elementAt( index ); }

protected final void put(Object obj)
{ elements_.addElement(obj); }
}
```

Notice that we have given CollectionImpl default package scope as we only want classes within this package to know about it. In this case, as in most, we have made the Vector instance variable private and provided protected helper methods for adding and retrieving elements. The rationale behind the decision to make elements_ a private and not a protected instance variable is to allow us to "upgrade" CollectionImpl at a later date without impacting on its subclasses. That is, we could easily replace the Vector instance variable with an alternative collection class at a later date without having to rewrite any of CollectionImpl's subclasses.

Given the above class we can rewrite StringVector to extend CollectionImpl, thus getting the common delegated methods for free.

```
public class StringVector extends CollectionImpl
{
  public void addElement(String str)
  {
    put( str ); //using protected method
  }
  public String elementAt( int index )
  {
    return (String)get( index );
  }
  //isEmpty() etc. public in CollectionImpl
}
```

Having migrated the common behavior and instance variables into class CollectionImpl we can easily go about the business of writing other typesafe homogenous collection classes. For example, here is DateVector:

```
public class DateVector extends CollectionImpl
{
  public void addElement(Date date)
  {
    put( date );
  }
  public Date elementAt( int index )
  {
    return (Date)get( index );
  }
}
```

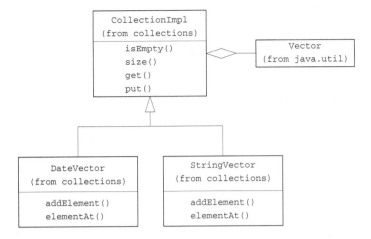

Figure 10.1 Typesafe collection using generalization and delegation

Figure 10.1 shows how it all hangs together in UML.

Runtime typed collections

An alternative approach to writing homogenous collections is to defer the type checking to runtime and throw an exception when the wrong class of object is added to the collection. Compile-time type checking is always preferable to runtime type checking; however, there are always trade-offs to be considered. In this case the trade-off is between reusability and runtime safety. In some cases runtime safety may not be such an issue as any inconsistencies in the objects being added to a runtime typed collection could easily be picked up during the development life cycle – assuming that you test your code!

To be able to write a generic/reusable homogenous collection that checks the class of the object being added at runtime, we need a mechanism to determine the type of object. In this case the instanceof operator is not going to be of much help as we want to write a generic class. If you have been steadily working your way through this book you should be more than familiar with Java's Class object by now.

Here is our first attempt at writing a runtime typed collection. First we define an exception class to throw if the wrong class of object is added to the collection, followed by our new collection class which extends CollectionImp listed above.

```
class WrongClassException extends Exception
{
  public WrongClassException(String what)
  { super(what); }
}
```

```
public class RuntimeTypedVector extends CollectionImpl
{
  private Class class_;

  public RuntimeTypedVector(Class c)
  {  class_=c;    }

  public void addElement(Object obj)
    throws WrongClassException
  {
    Class c=obj.getClass();
    if(c!=class_)
      throw new WrongClassException(""+c);

    //correct class type
    put( obj );
  }
  public Object elementAt(int index)
  {
    return get(index);
  }
}
```

The class `RuntimeTypedVector` is constructed with a `Class` object instance as follows:

```
RuntimeTypedVector rtv =
  new RuntimeTypedVector(String.class);
```

The `Class` parameter to the constructor is cached and then used to do a comparison with the class of the object parameter `obj` in `addElement()`. To see how this works at runtime we will try to add an `Integer` to an instance of `RuntimeTypedVector` instantiated with `String.class`.

```
RuntimeTypedVector rtv=
  new RuntimeTypedVector(String.class);

try
{
  rtv.addElement( "String" );        //okay
  rtv.addElement( new Integer(10) ); //will throw exception
}
catch(WrongClassException ex)
{ ex.printStackTrace(); }
```

The output from the above example is:

```
WrongClassException: class java.lang.Integer
  at RuntimeTypedVector.addElement(RuntimeTypedVector.java)
```

So there you have it – a generic runtime typed collection class. Well, almost. There is still one problem to overcome before we have a truly generic `RuntimeTypedVector` class. As it stands, we cannot add subclasses of the class parameter passed to RuntimeTypedVector without it throwing a WrongClassException. This is bad news because clients of RuntimeTypedVector would expect to be able to use it as follows:

```
RuntimeTypedVector rtv=
    new RuntimeTypedVector(Component.class);

try
{
    rtv.addElement( new Panel() );    //will throw exception
    rtv.addElement( new Canvas()) );  //will throw exception
}
catch(WrongClassException ex)
{ ex.printStackTrace(); }
```

The reason addElement() throws an exception is because it only checks the class of the parameter against the Class that RuntimeTypedVector was constructed with. So in the case of rtv.addElement(new Panel()) the expression if(c!=class_) is equivalent to if(Panel.class != Component.class) which evaluates to true, therefore addElement()proceeds by throwing an exception.

Fortunately this is easy to resolve by using one of the new methods in class Class introduced in Java 1.1, namely isAssignableFrom().

```
public class RuntimeTypedVector extends CollectionImpl
{
    private Class class_;

    public RuntimeTypedVector(Class c)
    { class_=c; }

    public void addElement(Object obj)
        throws WrongClassException
    {
        if(class_.isAssignableFrom(obj.getClass())==false)
            throw new WrongClassException(""+obj.getClass());

        //correct class type
        put( obj );
    }
    public Object elementAt(int index)
    {
        return get(index);
    }
}
```

This will allow us to instantiate a RuntimeTypedVector with either a superclass or an interface. So given the following class hierarchy:

```
interface ParallelPortDevice {}
class Printer implements ParallelPortDevice {}
class InkJetPrinter extends Printer{}
```

we can instantiate RuntimeTypedVector with ParallelPortDevice.class and add instances of Printer or InkJetPrinter without addElement() throwing an exception.

```
RuntimeTypedVector rtv=
  new RuntimeTypedVector(ParallelPortDevice.class);

rtv.addElement( new Printer() );
rtv.addElement( new InkJetPrinter() );
rtv.addElement( new String("str") ); //throws exception
```

If you are using Java 1.02 you will have to write your own version of isAssignableFrom() by utilizing isInterface(), getSuperClass() and getInterfaces() to check the super types of the class. Here is an example implementation:

```
public final class ClassAssistant
{
  public static boolean isAssignableFrom(Class from,Class to)
  {
    Class c=to;
    if(from.isInterface())
    {
      while(c!=null)
      {
        Class [] ifc=c.getInterfaces();
        int num=ifc.length;
        for(int i=0;i<num;i++)
        {
          if(ifc[i]==from)
          {
            return true;
          }
        }
        c=c.getSuperclass();
      }
      return false;
    }
    else
    {
      while(c!=from )
      {
        //check superclasses
        c=c.getSuperclass();
        if(c==null)
        {
          return false;
        }
      }
    }
```

```
        return true;
    }
  }
}

//Java 1.02 version of
//RuntimeTypedVector.addElement()

public void addElement(Object obj)
  throws WrongClassException
{
  if(ClassAssistant.isAssignableFrom(class_,obj.getClass()))
    put( obj );
  else
    throw new WrongClassException
      ("Invalid class "+obj.getClass());
}
```

Here are the pros and cons of the two approaches examined thus far:

Idiom	Benefits	Disadvantages
Compile typesafe collection	Compiler does the checking	Increased number of classes and impacts on the overall size of a system
Runtime typed collection	Reusable, does not impact on the overall size of a system	Risk of runtime exceptions. Slower adding elements as their classes have to be checked

Both the above idioms can be very effective; however, we can achieve the same goals though encapsulation without any of the disadvantages listed above.

Earlier we wrote a FavoriteURLVector class to avoid the problems associated with heterogeneous collections classes such as Vector. Let us now look at the problem from a different perspective.

We have been asked to write a class that can manage FavoriteURL objects and provide a range of services, such as sorting, to its clients. Using the typesafe homogenous idiom we could write a class like this:

```
public class URLManager
{
  private FavoriteURLVector urls_ =
    new FavoriteURLVector();

  public void add(FavoriteURL url)
  { urls_.addElement( url ); }
```

```
public FavoriteURL get(int index)
{ return urls_.elementAt( index ); }

public void sortByName()
{ /*sort the vector*/ }
}
```

If you examine URLManager you will see that we have provided public methods written in terms of FavoriteURL objects. So why do we need FavoriteURLVector? The simple answer is that we do not!

We can achieve the same effect simply by encapsulating a Vector within URLManager and placing the type safety in public methods, without the overhead of an additional class.

```
public class URLManager
{

  private Vector urls_ = new Vector();

  public void add(FavoriteURL url) //typesafe
  { urls_.addElement( url ); }

  public FavoriteURL get(int index)
  { return (FavoriteURL)urls_.elementAt( index ); }

  public void sortByName()
  { /*sort the vector*/}
}
```

Generally we prefer this technique to the runtime typed idiom, but this still leaves us with one problem. What should we do if another class needs to access the list of FavoriteURL objects, when we do not want the other class to become dependent on URLManager?

If we were to provide an accessor method to return the internal Vector we are opening the door again to the risk of clients adding Spanner objects. We could solve that by making URLManager return a "read-only" interface, but there is a more elegant solution in the form of iterators, which allow us to do this and much more without breaking encapsulation and coupling clients to the kind of collection class being used. Iterators are examined in the next chapter.

SUMMARY

Almost all non-trivial programs use collection classes in one form or other.

Collections should hide any underlying implementation details that may be used to implement their behavior. As we will see in the next chapter, iterators can be used to extend and enforce these design goals.

Java's heterogeneous collection classes such as Vector may at first sight appear to be dangerous owing to the risk of runtime cast errors. However, through the careful use of encapsulation you can achieve type safety without the excessive use of homogenous collection classes.

Other object-oriented languages such as Eiffel and C++ have parameterized classes which their respective compilers can use to generate homogenous collections – often referred to as static polymorphism. A great deal of debate has taken place within the Java community as to whether parameterized features should be introduced into the language; however, it has been our experience that using homogenous but typesafe collection classes enforces type safety, leading to robust runtime systems, but also deals with the code bloat and compile-time problems that are encountered in the majority of type parameterized systems.

11 Iterators

The power of iterators

Types of iterators

Multi-threading

Introduction

Iterators cannot really exist without collections, so if you are reading this chapter before you have had a look at the chapter on collections, we suggest that you go back to catch up before wading too deeply into the iterators stream.

When dealing with collection classes, iterators are there to provide an abstract mechanism by which to access elements in collection classes, without revealing the underlying implementation or the data structure being used.

The power of iterators

We have used iterators before in some of our examples, most notably `java.util.Enumeration` in the `Employee` pay model in Chapter 3. `java.lang.Vector` returns an iterator via its method `elements()` in the form of an `Enumeration`. Here is the Java definition of an enumeration:

```
public interface java.util.Enumeration
{
  public abstract boolean hasMoreElements();
  public abstract Object nextElement();
}
```

To illustrate the power of iterators we are first going to consider what we see as a poorly encapsulated code example and then suggest improvements that you may wish to apply in order to correct it.

Assume that we have added a `getVector()` method to the `URLManager` class that we used in the previous chapter. This method allows us to pass the `Vector` to the method `populateList()` shown below:

```
public class FavoritesEditor extends Frame
{
  private List favorites_= new List();

  public FavoritesEditor()
  { super("Favorites editor"); }

  public void populateList( Vector urls )
  {
    //Bad use of iterator
    Enumeration iter= urls.elements();
    while(iter.hasMoreElements())
    {
      FavoriteURl url= (FavoriteURl)iter.nextElement();
      String item= url.getDescription()+" "+url.getURL();
      favorites_.addItem( item );
    }
  }
}

//client code

FavoritesEditor editor= new FavoritesEditor();
URLManager urlman= new URLManager();
//add some favorites
//pass vector to editor
editor.populateList( urlman.getVector() );
```

So why is this so poorly encapsulated? `FavoritesEditor` is not coupled to `URLManager` and that is a good start, but consider the implication if you decided to modify `URLManager` to use a `Hashtable` instead of a `Vector`. Everywhere you have written code which uses the `getVector()` method will have to be modified, as will the `populateList()` method.

To improve on the above design we can rewrite `populateList()` to take an `Enumeration` parameter instead of a `Vector`; that way any collection class supporting a `FavoriteURL` iterator can be used.

```
public void populateList(Enumeration iter )
{
  while(iter.hasMoreElements())
  {
    FavoriteURL url= (FavoriteURL)iter.nextElement();
    String item= url.getDescription()+" "+url.getURL();
    favorites_.addItem( item );
  }
}
```

To show how flexible this new design is, we are first going to update `URLManager` to support iteration by providing an `elements()` method instead of the `getVector()`

method and then write a simple adapter class that allows us to iterate over an array via an Enumeration.

```
//updated URLManager supporting Enumeration
public class URLManager
{
  private Vector urls_ = new Vector();
  //add() and get() as before

  public Enumeration elements()
  {
    return urls_.elements(); //using delegation
  }
}

//Generic Array adapter class providing an Enumeration
public class ArrayAdapter
{
  private Object [] array_;

  //inner class impl of Enumeration
  private class ArrayEnum
    implements java.util.Enumeration
  {
    private int cursor_;

    public boolean hasMoreElements()
    { return cursor_<array_.length;}

    public Object nextElement()
    { return array_[cursor_++];    }
  }

  public ArrayAdapter(Object [] array)
  { array_=array;}

  public java.util.Enumeration elements()
  { return new ArrayEnum() ; }
}
```

The sample client code below illustrates how we can now pass the elements into populateList() from any FavoriteURL source, in this case either from URLManager or via the ArrayAdapter.

```
//sample client code
FavoriteUrl [] urls= new FavoriteURL[2];
URLManager urlman= new URLManager();

FavoriteURL url1=new FavoriteURL( ... );
FavoriteURL url2=new FavoriteURL( ... );
```

```
urls[0]=url1; //add to the array
urls[1]=url2;

urlman.add( url1 ); //add to URLManager
urlman.add( url2 );

//create an instance of our ArrayAdapter
ArrayAdapter array= new ArrayAdapter( urls );

//create an instance of FavoriteEditor
FavoritesEditor editor= new FavoritesEditor();

//either use ArrayAdapter or URLManager
editor.populateList( urlman.elements() );
editor.populateList( array.elements() );
```

By using iterators we can design classes and subsystems that are loosely coupled, allowing us to update the type of collection classes used without affecting client classes that depend on their data. We have almost come back full circle to the start of the whole area of collections, in that we were looking at heterogeneous collection classes and how to avoid their pitfalls, as we now have heterogeneous iterators in the form of java.util.Enumeration. We can apply the same encapsulation rules that we used before to enforce type safety at subsystem or class boundaries.

Or, to put it another way, type safety is most important in interfaces. Classes that use heterogeneous collections privately and never expose their data can easily manage the casting from Object with little or no risk; however, if that class provides a public interface to an iterator you should consider making the iterator homogenous. For example, the method populateList() is public, but not typesafe, which means that an Enumeration can be passed in, regardless of the type of objects it contains.

To conclude our introduction to iterators we are going to improve the above classes one more time to make them more robust and typesafe. populateList() has been updated as follows:

```
public void populateList(FavURLIterator iter ) {...}
```

Here is the new typesafe iterator for FavoriteURL objects:

```
public interface FavURLIterator
{
  public boolean hasMoreElements();
  public FavoriteURL nextElement();
}
```

There are several ways we could modify URLManager to provide FavURLIterator. For this example we have used a private inner class; however, we could have declared URLManager as implementing FavURLIterator and delegated to elements_ in the implementation, reducing the need for an additional class.

```
//updated URLManager with homogenous iterator
public class URLManager
```

```
{
  //as before
  private class Iterator
    implements FavURLIterator
  {
    public boolean hasMoreElements()
    { return elements_.hasMoreElements();}
    public FavoriteURL nextElement()
    { return (FavoriteURL)elements_.nextElement();}
  }

  public FavURLIterator elements()
  {
    return new Iterator();
  }
}
```

With this final version any attempts to pass Enumerations of Spanner objects into FavoriteURLEditor would be ruled out by the compiler.

Types of iterators

Iterators come in many flavors and combinations of behavior. A basic set of iterators would include many permutation of the following behavior:

- Forward
- Reverse
- Insert
- Delete
- Read

For example, VectorEnumeration is a *Forward*-only *Read*-only iterator.

Uni-directional iterators

Uni-directional iterators only permit the traversal of their underlying data structures in a single direction, either *forward* or *reverse*. At their simplest, uni-directional iterators start life pointing to either the first or last element and then allow traversal to the opposite end.

Forward iterator

In the case of Vector, its Enumeration (class VectorEnumeration) starts at the first element and allows forward iteration via nextElement(), making it a forward-only iterator. As the Enumeration interface does not specify a remove() or insert() we can also state that it is a read-only iterator. The inner class ArrayEnum in the ArrayAdapter class above also implements Enumeration as a read-only forward iterator.

Reverse iterator

Reverse iterators allow traversal of their underlying data structures from a known element, often the last one in the collection, in a reverse order, similar to using an array as follows: array[index--]. We can therefore update our ArrayAdapter class to provide a reverse iterator by writing another inner class that implements the Enumeration interface, but decrements its internal cursor_ on each call to nextElement().

```
public class ArrayAdapter
{
  //as before
  private class ReverseArrayEnum
    implements Enumeration
  {
    private int cursor_;

    public ReverseArrayEnum()
    { cursor_=array_.length-1;} //position cursor_ at end
    public boolean hasMoreElements()
    { return cursor_>=0;} //check we're not before the start
    public Object nextElement()
    { return array_[cursor_--]; } //get previous element
  }

  public ReverseEnumeration reverseElements()
  { return new ReverseArrayEnum() ; }
}
```

Now that class ArrayAdapter supports both forward and reverse iteration we can use it as follows:

```
public class IterTest
{
  static public void main(String [] args )
  {
    ArrayAdapter adapter= new ArrayAdapter( args );

    printElements( adapter.elements() ); //forward iteration
    printElements( adapter.reverseElements() ); //reverse
  }
  static void printElements( java.util.Enumeration e )
  {
    while(e.hasMoreElements() )
```

```
    {
      System.out.println( e.nextElement() );
    }
    System.out.println("** END **");
  }
}
```

In the example above, the code in `main()` simply instantiates an `ArrayAdapter` with the command line arguments, `args []`, and calls the method `printElements()` first with the forward iterator followed by a call with the reverse iterator. The example code produces the following output:

```
>java IterTest first second

first
second
** END **
second
first
** END **
```

Bi-directional iterators

Bi-directional iterators allow traversal in both directions, supporting the equivalent of a `nextElement()` and a `previousElement()` method. Sticking with our `ArrayAdapter` class, we can support bi-directional iteration by declaring a new interface `BiEnumeration` which extends `Enumeration`:

```
interface BiEnumeration
  extends java.util.Enumeration,
{
  public Object previousElement();
  public void positionAtStart();
  public void positionAtEnd();
}
```

Before writing any implementation class in a hierarchy it is worth considering if there are any candidates for reuse or if generalization/specialization can be applied to any existing classes without impacting on any existing code. In this case we are about to implement a bi-directional iterator, so how should we go about using generalization/specialization?

If you examine the interface signature for `BiEnumeration` you will see that it implements `Enumeration`, meaning that anywhere an `Enumeration` is expected we can use a `BiEnumeration`. Keeping that in mind, we can ditch the inner classes `ArrayEnum` and `ReverseArrayEnum` and use a `BiEnumeration` instead.

Below is the inner class which behaves as either an `Enumeration` (forward/reverse) or a `BiEnumeration`:

```
private class BiArrayEnum
  implements BiEnumeration
{
  private int cursor_;
  private boolean reverseIter;

  public BiArrayEnum(int start)
  {
    cursor_=start; //set the starting position
  }
  public BiArrayEnum(boolean reverse)
  {
    //act as reverse iterator
    //to replace ReverseEnum
    cursor_=array_.length-1;
    isReverseIter=reverse;
  }
  public boolean hasMoreElements()
  { return cursor_<array_.length && cursor_>=0;}
  public Object nextElement()
  {
    if(isReverseIter) //reverse iter
      return previousElement();
    return array_[cursor_++];
  }
  public Object previousElement()
  { return array_[cursor_--]; }
  public void positionAtStart()
  { cursor_=0; }
  public void positionAtEnd()
  { cursor_=array_.length-1;}
}
```

Now all we need to is to update the ArrayAdapter class to instantiate an instance of BiArrayEnum instead of ArrayEnum and ReverseEnum, making sure we position cursor_ at the correct location (0) and pass in the isReverseIter flag respectively.

```
//ArrayAdapter
// iterator methods all instantiate a BiArrayEnum
public java.util.Enumeration elements()
{ return new BiArrayEnum(0) ; } //position at start
public BiEnumeration biElements()
{ return new BiArrayEnum(0);} //position at start
public Enumeration reverseElements()
{ return new BiArrayEnum(true) ; } //flag as reverse
```

Here is an updated version of class `IterTest` that uses the three type iterators:

```
public class IterTest
{
  static public void main(String [] args )
  {
    ArrayAdapter adapter= new ArrayAdapter( args );

    printElements( adapter.elements() ); //forward
    printElements( adapter.reverseElements() ); //reverse
    printElements( adapter.biElements() ); //bi
    biPrintElements( adapter.biElements() ); //bi
  }

  static void printElements( java.util.Enumeration e )
  {
    while(e.hasMoreElements() )
    {
      System.out.println( e.nextElement() );
    }
    System.out.println("** END **");
  }
  static void biPrintElements( BiEnumeration e )
  {
    e.positionAtEnd();
    while(e.hasMoreElements() )
    {
      System.out.println( e.previousElement() );
    }
    System.out.println("** END **");
    //reuse printElements() above
    e.positionAtStart();
    printElements( e );
  }
}
```

A UML diagram for the complete `ArrayAdapter` is shown in Figure 11.1.

Other types of iterator

So far we have described read-only iterators; both uni-directional and bi-directional iterators can also be updatable. That is, clients can insert, replace, and remove elements from the underlying collection class. All these iterators are known as external iterators as the iteration takes place outside of the collection class. There is, you guessed it, another type of iterator – the internal iterator, and that is what we are going to investigate next.

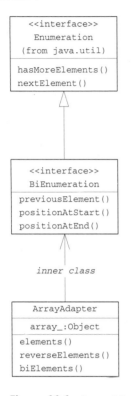

Figure 11.1 ArrayAdapter

Internal iterators

Internal iterators are not like their external cousins in that client classes have no knowledge of their interfaces, and they cannot control the iteration process. Collection classes often use internal iterators to allow clients to apply some "function" to each of its internal elements. It may seem strange that in a book about object-oriented idioms we suddenly introduce the word "function." Trust us, there is a good reason for its usage in the context of internal iterators. Internal iterators can be used to implement part of the Visitor design pattern, where objects "visit" elements in a data structure.

Functors

To implement an internal iterator for a collection class we need to be able to pass a "function" to an instance of that class so it can apply it to each of its elements. As Java is an object-oriented language and does not have stand-alone functions (fortunately), how are we going to be able to do this?

This is where Functors enter the picture. In Java a Functor is an object that acts like a function, that is, it has no state and performs a specific task only. The best way to implement Functors in Java is by using interfaces. Below is an interface for a generic Functor:

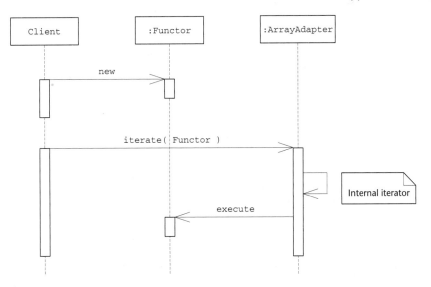

Figure 11.2 Functor interaction diagram

```
public interface Functor
{
    public Object execute( Object object );
}
```

To see how Functors work with internal iterators we have added the method iterate() to our ArrayAdapter class.

```
public void iterate( Functor functor )
{
    //iterate internally
    //pass element at cursor position
    //to functor

    int len=array_.length;
    for( int i=0;i<len;i++)
    {
        array_[i]=functor.execute( array_[i] );
    }
}
```

If you examine iterate() you will see that it invokes execute() on the Functor for each of its elements and assigns the return value back to that element, allowing the Functor to modify or change the object – in effect allowing the ArrayAdapter to support updatable iteration. Figure 11.2 is an interaction diagram illustrating how the Functor works.

We now have a very generic model where any Functor can be used on any type of object. Here is an example where we have passed the command line arguments to the ArrayAdapter and then used a Functor to reverse the String objects:

```
class StrRevFunctor
  implements Functor
{
  public Object execute( Object object )
  {
    StringBuffer buf= new StringBuffer((String)object);
    buf.reverse();
    return buf.toString();
  }
}

public class FunctorTest
{
  static public void main( String [] args)
  {
    ArrayAdapter array= new ArrayAdapter( args );

    printElements( array.elements() );
    //apply Functor
    array.iterate( new StrRevFunctor() );
    //print again
    printElements( array.elements() );
  }
  static void printElements( java.util.Enumeration e )
  {
    while(e.hasMoreElements() )
    {
      System.out.println( e.nextElement() );
    }
    System.out.println("** END **");
  }
}
```

This produces the following output:

```
>java FunctorTest hello goodbye
hello
goodbye
** END **
olleh
eybdoog
** END **
```

Internal iterators with callbacks

Another interesting application of internal iterators is to use them to reduce client code duplication. The generic pseudo code for using an external iterator such as `Enumeration` is as follows:

1. while enumeration has more elements
2. get next element
3. process element

so everywhere you use an external iterator you will end up writing code that loops through the elements in an Enumeration, getting the next element and proceeding by processing that element in some fashion. So the aim here is to factor this code into an internal iterator – as we did for the Functor. The only difference between the Functor implementation and a callback internal iterator is that the underlying elements are not altered by the client – a read-only iterator. The last piece of the jigsaw is to define a new interface to use as a parameter to a new method in the `ArrayAdapter` class.

```java
public interface ElementConsumer
{
  public void processElement(Object obj);
}

//new method in ArrayAdapter
public void iterate(ElementConsumer consumer)
{
  //iterate internally
  //pass element at cursor position
  //to the ElementConsumer

  int len=array_.length;
  for( int i=0;i<len;i++)
  {
    //callback with each element
    consumer.processElement(array_[i]);
  }
}
```

The new `iterate()` method is using a synchronous callback to the `consumer` object passed in as a parameter. Below is some sample client code where class `TestConsumer` simply prints the contents of each element to `System.out`:

```java
class TestConsumer
   implements ElementConsumer
{
  public void processElement(Object obj)
  {
    System.out.println( obj );
  }
}
```

```
public class InternalIteratorTest
{
   static public void main( String [] args)
   {
     ArrayAdapter array= new ArrayAdapter( args );

     TestConsumer c= new TestConsumer();
     //iterate calls back with each element
     array.iterate( c );

   }
}
```

With the following command line:

```
>java InternalIteratorTest arg1 arg2 arg3
```

the above code will produce the output:

```
arg1
arg2
arg3
```

Observable iterators and collections

The callback internal iterator is almost, but not quite, implementing an Observer/Observable model. The Observer pattern can, however, be combined with an iterator to create an Observable iterator or indeed be used by a collection class to inform its observers if an element is added, removed, or the collection is altered in any other way.

Multi-threading

Just to finish up on iterators it is important to discuss some uses of iterators in a multi-threaded environment.

The basic problem with using iterators that are shared, or for that matter collections that are shared, is that it is hard to keep all of the parts of the system up to date with one another. A simple solution to this problem is that we use synchronization on the collection class that we are using to store data and lock the class with the standard Java object locking mechanisms.

This is fine until we return an iterator. At this stage we can consider two possible approaches. One approach is for the iterator to take a complete copy of the contents of the collection before the iterator is returned to the client software.

This is sometimes referred to as a snapshot iterator, in that it is like taking a picture of the state of the collection at the time of the call and then returning the complete picture of the collection in the iterator. This is a relatively simple solution, because from this point on, the iterator is no longer connected to the collection in any way.

In this case a thread that has taken an iterator simply sees a picture of the state of the collection as it was at the time the collection was asked for the iterator, so there is never a problem if we are not worried about how up to date the iterator is when we finally get to use it.

However, we have paid a very heavy price in terms of processor and memory usage in order to achieve this simplicity. In some cases, when the amount of objects in the collection is very large and the number of client threads taking snapshots of the collection is very large, we could just spend all our days taking pictures of our collection which never has any time to be updated. So copying the full collection every time is just not a workable solution. In this case the iterator must stay connected to the collection in order to have access to its contained objects, so that we can avoid the copying problems.

Another approach which can sometimes help to avoid synchronization problems associated with shared iterators or collections is to use the Observer pattern. In this model, clients of a collection or iterator are notified if the collection changes in any way, thus eliminating the need for several threads to be querying a collection concurrently. This approach will not get you out of jail for all designs, but can often reduce the complexity of an object model requiring asynchronous updates.

SUMMARY

Iterators provide an abstract mechanism for accessing elements in collection classes, without revealing the underlying implementation or the data structure being used by the collection class. In almost all designs it is preferable to pass iterators between different client classes or subsystems rather than passing, say, a Vector or Hashtable.

By rethinking your designs to be based around iterators rather than their collection class, you can reduce the dependencies between classes and open the door for a collection class to be replaced at a later date with no impact on the client code.

External, forward-only, read-only iterators such as Enumeration are the "bread and butter" of the iterator world. Functor, callback, and observable iterators are powerful idioms, but be careful to use them in the correct context, that is, think carefully about your design before using them.

All designs become more complex when multiple threads are introduced, so be careful when using iterators and collections extensively in this context. Consider whether a simpler and cleaner model, such as the Observer pattern, can be used to provide asynchronous updates or whether "snapshot" iterators can be used.

Appendix A:
Diagrams and coding
conventions

Introduction to UML

In this section we will be taking a brief look at the notation we have used for the diagrams that accompany the code examples, namely UML. Short for Unified Modeling Language, UML is a convergence of the three main notations that are used in the methodologies of Booch, OMT, and OOSE. Although we are personally sad to see Booch's "clouds" omitted from UML we feel that a single unified modeling language is a big step forward in the Object community and one that we should embrace. This section is not intended as a complete guide to UML, but as more of an overview to how we use a small subset of the modeling language to illustrate the designs in this book. See References for further reading.

UML is a general-purpose notational language for specifying, visualizing, constructing, and documenting the artifacts of object-oriented software systems. We use two types of UML diagrams to aid the visualization of the code examples in this book: class diagrams and object interaction diagrams. Do not worry if you are not familiar with object-oriented modeling languages as the notation used for both class and object interaction diagrams is very easy to pick up. There is a wide range of software packages available to aid the use of UML. Initially we used Rational's *Rose for Java* edition to produce the diagrams in this book.

Class diagrams

At its simplest, a class diagram can be used to show relationships, such as inheritance or aggregation, between different classes. Before looking at how these relationships are represented in UML, let us briefly look at the notation for a Java class. A class is represented by a box divided into three sections:

- Class name
- Fields (instance variables)
- Methods

Using the Java class below as an example, the UML class could be shown as in Figure A.1. Keep in mind that you can show as much or as little information about the class as you choose. Sometimes too much information can make a diagram harder to understand, as can too little.

```
┌─────────────────────────┐
│        UMLClass         │
├─────────────────────────┤
│    intField_            │
│    $ staticField        │
├─────────────────────────┤
│    method1()            │
│    method2()            │
└─────────────────────────┘
```

Figure A.1

```
public class UMLClass
{
    private int intField_;
    private static int staticField_;

    public void method1() {}
    public void method2() {}
}
```

Diagram supporting text

Comments and supporting text are shown using the following icon:

Comments

Inheritance

Inheritance is shown in a class diagram by a solid line with an arrow from a subclass to its superclass with the arrow head pointing at the superclass.

So given the Java code:

```
public class Printer extends ParallelPortPeripheral
{ ... }
```

the UML class diagram would be as shown in Figure A.2.

Figure A.2

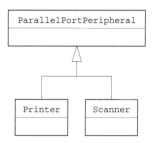

Figure A.3

When we have more that one subclass we show the relationship by joining the lines rather than having multiple single lines from the subclasses to their superclass, as shown in Figure A.3.

Java interfaces

Although there is no direct support for interfaces in UML, we can use a stereotype to indicate in our class diagrams that what appears to be a superclass is in fact an interface. Java interfaces are shown using the notation <<interface>> (Figure A.4).

```java
public interface Peripheral
{
  public boolean commTest();
  public String vendorInfo();
}

public class ParallelPortPeripheral
  implements Peripheral
{
  public boolean commTest() {...}
  public String vendorInfo() {...}
}
```

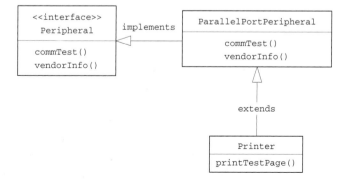

Figure A.4

```
public class Printer
        extends ParallelPortPeripheral
{
  public void printTestPage() {...}
}
```

Aggregation

We use aggregation in our examples to represent the "has a" relationship. So given the following classes, where a Computer "has a" Keyboard:

```
public class Keyboard {...}

public class Computer
{
    private Keyboard keyboard_ = new Keyboard();
    //...
}
```

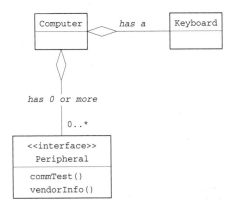

Figure A.5

In UML the *has a* relationship would be modelled by a solid line with a diamond pointing at the containing class (Figure A.5).

We can also indicate cardinality by adding a number at one or both ends of the aggregation notation. Assuming the Computer class has zero or more Peripherals we can update the code and Figure A.5 as follows (Figure A.6):

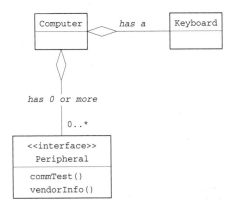

Figure A.6

```
public class Computer
{
  private Keyboard keyboard_ = new Keyboard();
  private Peripheral [] peripheral_;
//
}
```

Notice that the notation 0..* has been added to the class diagram to show the cardinality, that is, Computer has zero or more Peripherals. This is one of many cardinality relationships that can be defined in UML. Common examples include one–one, one–many and many–many relationships.

Dependency

If a class has a dependency on another class or interface, a dotted line is used between the two dependent classes. Additionally an arrow can be used to indicate the direction of the dependency. The dependency notation is used to represent the "uses" relationship as opposed to the "has a" described above.

Sticking with the Peripheral hierarchy we are going to declare a new class PeripheralTester which is dependent on the interface Peripheral. In this case PeripheralTester is dependent on Peripheral, so we indicate this by the direction of the arrow (Figure A.7).

```
public class PeripheralTester
{
  public void test( Peripheral p ) {...}
}
```

To conclude the brief introduction to UML class diagrams, Figure A.8 shows a UML diagram pulling all the previous examples together.

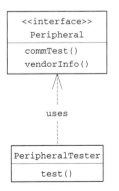

Figure A.7

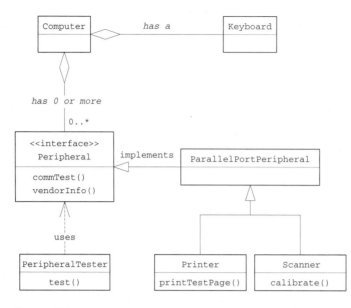

Figure A.8

Interaction diagrams

Object Interaction Diagrams (OIDs) are used to show how objects interact at runtime. So given the implementation code for the PeripheralTester.test() method we can produce the UML OID shown in Figure A.9.

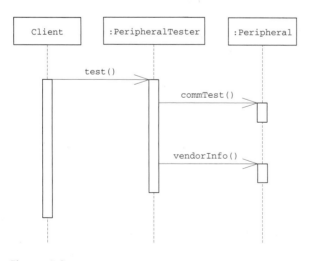

Figure A.9

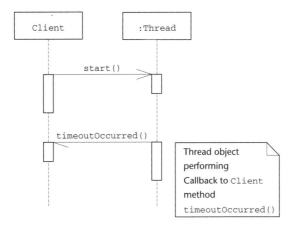

Figure A.10

```
public class PeripheralTester
{
  public void test( Peripheral p )
  {
    boolean online=p.commTest();
    String vendor=p.vendorInfo();
    //etc.
  }
}
```

The direction of the arrow indicates which object is the sender and which is the receiver of the message. Although we could have included lines to show the return from each interaction, it is generally implicit, so we reserve its usage for asynchronous messages. Asynchronous interactions are shown as in Figure A.10 and apply to concurrent implementations – those using multiple threads. The interaction diagram in Figure A.10 shows an object called Client invoking start() on an instance of Thread which, in turn, performs an asynchronous callback to Client method timeoutOccurred().

Notice that the asynchronous message has the upper portion of the arrow head removed.

UML covers much more than illustrated above; however, to make the diagrams in this book as accessible as possible we have limited our usage of UML.

Code naming conventions

Deciding upon a code naming convention for an organization can be fraught with conflicting options and vested interests; rarely will anybody involved in the process willingly volunteer to drop their favorite coding style in favor of somebody else's. The main reason for deciding on a coding convention is consistency, so any developer within an organization can easily follow another person's code. In our case we needed consistency throughout a book, so before we started to write this book we too had to go through this process. Fortunately diplomacy prevailed and no blood was spilt. After several long debates on the subject we opted for using a coding convention that neither of us had used before. We decided to base our coding convention around Doug Lea's naming conventions (Lea, 1997). Doug's naming convention for instance variables is quite different than anything we have used before, but like most of the conventions we have had to adopt in the past, we soon became used to it as it gradually assimilated our code examples. Listed below are the conventions, followed by a class example.

Packages

```
lowercase
```

Interface

```
UpperAndLowerCase
```

Class names

```
UpperAndLowerCase
```

or to distinguish from an interface:

```
InterfaceNameImpl
```

Abstract classes

```
UpperAndLowerCase
```

or to distinguish from an interface:

```
AbstractInterfaceName
```

Exception class

```
ClassNameEndsWithException
ReallyLongClassNameEndsWithEx
```

Constants

```
UPPER_CASE_WITH_UNDERSCORES
```

Instance and class variables (fields)

```
trailingUnderscore_
```

Local variables

```
firstWordLowerCase
```

Methods

```
firstWordLowerCase()
```

Example

```
public class CodingConventionsImpl
  extends AbstractCodingConventions
  implements CodingConventions
{
  private int intField_;
  public static final int PUBLIC_CONSTANT= 0;

  public void methodThatThrowsException()
    throws CodingConventionException
  {...}

  public void methodWithLocalVariable(int [] array)
  {
    int numObjects=array.length;
  }
}
```

Appendix B:
Summary of rules,
design principles, and tips

Chapter 1

(P) Aim to make all of your instance variables private and provide accessor methods where necessary.

(P) Make accessor methods for instance variables "final."

(P) Only use protected instance variables or protected constructors in well-defined packages.

(P) Use packages constantly to manage complexity.

(P) If a class is only used within a package, make it package local (default visibility) to reduce system-level coupling.

(P) Prefer the use of packages over static inner classes.

(P) An inner class only makes sense, and should only be used, if it is going to associate and be visible only to the class that contains it.

Chapter 2

(R) Constructors are not inherited.

(P) Keep inheritance hierarchies small.

(P) Prefer delegation or using utility classes over inheritance for reuse.

P Inheritance is a class-based, "is a type of" relationship.

R All classes implicitly extend the class Object.

P Avoid unnecessary casting.

R Interfaces cannot define constructors.

P Program to an interface, not to an implementation.

P If a class is designed to be inherited, but it does not make sense to have an instance of the class, it should be defined as abstract.

P Abstract classes that contain only method signatures and static final fields should be declared as interfaces.

Chapter 3

R The JVM will always search up the inheritance hierarchy from the real class of the target object, in order to find the first match for the signature of the target method, no matter what the apparent type of the object is at the time of the call.

P Migrate common instance variables and concrete accessor methods to an abstract class that can lie between the interface and concrete classes in a hierarchy.

Chapter 4

T Get your compiler to check that constants passed as parameters are valid.

T Declare method parameters as final when you want to guard against meaningless object reference assignment.

P Use a read-only interface to make a mutable object act as immutable.

T Understand the difference between shallow and deep copying.

Chapter 5

P Catch as many exceptions as possible explicitly – avoid `catch(Exception)` as the only exception handler.

P Identify exception classes during the design phase.

P Avoid using `try{...}catch{...}` on a per method basis for all methods within a block.

T Separate fatal and non-fatal exception class hierarchies.

T Reduce the overall number of exception classes by categorizing them and using a constant (typesafe) to represent the condition.

P Never let exceptions propagate out of a `finally` block.

P Never declare `throws Exception`. Always use a subclass of `Exception`.

P Understand the implications of throwing exceptions in constructors.

P Use exceptions to indicate exceptional and error conditions, *not* to return values from methods.

Chapter 7

P Use constructor chaining to make constructor behavior and default values appear in only one place in the chain.

P Use private helper methods to avoid `super()` and `this()` conflicts in constructor chaining.

(T) Never call an abstract method from a constructor in an abstract class.

(R) Always call `super.finalize()` at the end of a `finalize()` method.

(R) Never call `finalize()` explicitly.

Chapter 8

(T) Be aware of the potential for class garbage collection with Singletons.

Chapter 9

(T) Consider lazy instantiation as a policy to reduce resource requirements.

(P) Avoid lazy instantiation for concrete Singleton classes.

(P) Make methods using lazy instantiation "thread safe," if they can be called either directly or indirectly by client classes.

(T) Use the double-check idiom to protect methods using lazy instantiation.

Glossary

Abstract class A class that cannot be instantiated. Subclasses must provide implementations for an abstract class's abstract methods in order to compile.

Abstract method A method declared as abstract does not contain a body. Any behavior can only be implemented in a subclass.

Abstraction (an) The characteristics of a class or class of objects.

Abstraction (process) The process of identifying clearly defined conceptual boundaries that denote the characteristics of an object-oriented model.

Accessor method A method that provides public access to an encapsulated instance field.

Association A relationship between classes. Implies a dependency.

Asynchronous An asynchronous method call may be made by a client object at any time. It is assumed that the exact time of any asynchronous call may not be known or predicted.

Base class A class that is the superclass of the class currently under consideration. It may be the class at the root of the class hierarchy.

Callback An object registers with another object, which calls back asynchronously when a particular condition occurs.

Cardinality The cardinal relationship between instances of one class and another. For example, one-to-many, many-to-many, 1-to-n, and so on.

Child class Another name for a subclass or derived class.

Class Describes the fields and behavior, or methods, for a particular set of objects. An object is an instance of a class.

Class diagram A visual representation of the relationships between classes in a software architecture.

Class variable A static class variable is shared by all instances of a class.

Client An object that uses the services provided by another object or set of objects.

Collection class A class implementing a dynamic data structure for storing and retrieving sets of objects.

Concrete class A class that can be instantiated. That is, it has no abstract methods.

Constant A variable representing a fixed value such as PI. Constants are usually declared as static and final. Also see Typesafe constant.

Constructor A special method that can only be called when you instantiate an object. Constructors have the same name as their containing class and can be overloaded.

Container An instance of a collection class. A container "contains" instances of other objects.

Delegation   Forwarding requests to another object which provides the behavior required in an implementation for a class.

Derived class   Also referred to as a subclass.

Dynamic binding   The determination of method calls is deferred to runtime and bound at the time of execution by name.

Encapsulation   Hiding the internal implementation and state of a class by providing a set of well-defined methods.

Exception   A method can throw an exception to indicate that an error or exceptional condition has occurred. Use exceptions in preference to returning error codes from methods.

Field   A field is declared as a member of a class. It is either a reference or a primitive type.

Final class   A class that cannot be subclassed. Explicitly shows that a class is complete and that none of its methods can be overridden.

Final method   A method declared as final cannot be overridden. It can however be overloaded.

Functor   A class generally without fields that acts as a function.

Generalization   The process of migrating common instance variables and methods "up" a class hierarchy into a common parent or superclass.

GOF   Gang of four. Refers to the authors of *Design Patterns*.

Heterogeneous collection   A collection class that can contain instances of any type of object – opposite to homogenous collection.

Homogenous collection   A collection class that can only contain instances of a single type of object – opposite to heterogeneous.

Implementation   The internal details of a class that should be encapsulated.

Inheritance   Defines an *is a type of* relationship between classes. A class that "extends" another class inherits its superclass fields and behavior.

Instance variable   Another name for a field.

Instantiate   The process of creating an object. Most commonly in Java, an object is instantiated by the use of the new keyword.

Interaction diagram   Also referred to as an OID (Object Interaction Diagram). A visual representation of how several objects interact at runtime.

Interface   Groups a related set of method signatures or operations. If a class that implements an interface provides method bodies for all the method signatures in the interface it is said to be a concrete class. If only a subset of the methods are implemented the class must be declared as abstract.

Iterator   An object that provides encapsulated access to the elements of a collection class.

Object   An object is an instance of a class. It has identity – in the form of a reference, state – values for fields, and behavior – defined in the class methods.

Overload   Methods with the same name in the same class hierarchy, but different parameters, are referred to as overloaded methods.

Override   A subclass overrides a method in a superclass by providing a different implementation. For a method to be overridden its method name, parameters, and return type must be the same as the method in the superclass. Not to be confused with overloading.

Parent class   Also referred to as a superclass.

Polymorphism   The ability for an object to vary its behavior depending on its type. Must be implemented and resolved by a runtime system.

Primitive type   A type already defined by the Java system as opposed to a class derived from `Object` or an array.

Server   A server object provides a set of services to its client objects.

Specialization   The process of specializing the behavior of a superclass by overriding the superclass's behavior. The inverse of the process of generalization.

Subclass   Also referred to as a derived class. A subclass extends a superclass and provides specialized behavior by overriding methods declared in its superclass.

Subsystem   A self-contained unit of software which performs a set of operations used by a system as a whole. Subsystems in Java can be dynamically substituted through the use of class loading.

Superclass   Provides implementations for common behavior in a class hierarchy. A subclass extends a superclass. Also referred to as a parent or base class.

Synchronized   A method declared as synchronized can only be entered by a single thread of execution at any one time. Objects and classes can also be synchronized.

Synchronous   Synchronous method invocations occur in a sequence.

Thread of execution   A Java program can contain many threads of execution within a single process. A scheduler is responsible for context switching between the threads.

Typesafe constant   A constant that is an instance of a class rather than a primitive type.

UML   Unified modeling language.

Utility class   A class which is declared with all its methods as static. A utility class is never instantiated.

References

Gamma E., Helm R., Johnson R. and Vlissides J. (1995) *Design Patterns – Elements of Reusable Object-Oriented Software*. Addison-Wesley. ISBN: 0-201-63361-2

Lea D. (1997) *Concurrent Programming in Java*. Addison-Wesley. ISBN: 0-201-69581-2

Meyers S. (1995) *More Effective C++*. Addison-Wesley. ISBN: 0-201-63371-x

Roberts S. and Heller P. (1998) *Java 1.1 Certification Study Guide*. Sybex. ISBN: 0-7821-2069-5

Further reading

Beck K. (1996) *Smalltalk Best Practice Patterns*. Prentice-Hall. ISBN: 0-13-476904-x

Booch G. (1994) *Object-Oriented Analysis and Design*. Benjamin/Cummings. ISBN: 0-8053-5340-2

Coplien J.O. (1992) *Advanced C++ Programming Styles & Idioms*. Addison-Wesley. ISBN: 0-201-54855-0

Fowler M. with Scott K. (1997) *UML Distilled*. Addison-Wesley. ISBN: 0-201-32563-2

Gabriel R.P. (1996) *Patterns of Software: tales from the software community*. Oxford University Press. ISBN: 0-195-10269-x

Grand M. (1997) *Java Language Reference*. O'Reilly. ISBN: 1-56592-204-2

Lindholm T. and Yellin F. (1996) *The Java Virtual Machine Specification*. Addison-Wesley. ISBN: 0-201-63452-x

Meyer B. (1988) *Object-Oriented Software Construction*. Prentice-Hall. ISBN: 0-13-629031-0

Index